SNOWSHOE ROUTES

Northern California

SNOWSHOE ROUTES

Northern California

MARC J. SOARES

THE MOUNTAINEERS BOOKS

Published by
The Mountaineers Books
1001 SW Klickitat Way, Suite 201
Seattle, WA 98134

Published simultaneously in Great Britain by Cordee, 3a DeMontfort Street, Leicester, England, LE1 7HD

Manufactured in the United States of America

Project Editor: Margaret Sullivan
Cover and book design: The Mountaineers Books
Layout: Jennifer LaRock Shontz
Mapmaker: Jennifer LaRock Shontz
Photographer: Marc Soares

Cover photograph: © Ken Redding/Corbis
Frontispiece: *Hat Creek and Sugarloaf Peak*

Library of Congress Cataloging-in-Publication Data
Soares, Marc J.
    Snowshoe routes, Northern California / Marc J. Soares.— 1st ed.
        p. cm.
Includes index.
    ISBN 0-89886-853-X (pbk.)
    1. Snowshoes and snowshoeing—California—Guidebooks. 2. Trails—California—Guidebooks. 3. California—Guidebooks. I. Title.
    GV853 .S62 2002
    796.9'2'09794—dc21

                                                        2002009046

Contents

—Dewey Pt

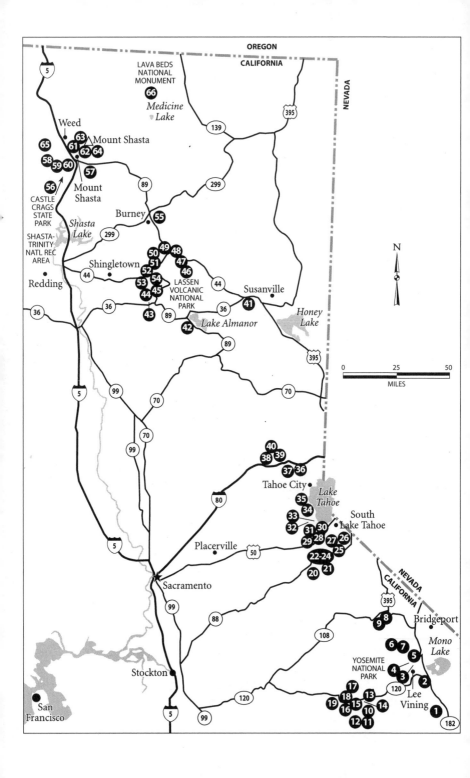

NORTHERN SIERRA NEVADA
Carson Pass Area near Highway 88   Kirkwood area

MAP KEY

————	paved road	●	city or town
═══════	dirt road	Ⓟ	parking
- - - - - - -	main trail	⛺	car campground
◄··············	other trail	⛺	backcountry campsite
+++++++++	railroad	⊼	picnic area
	boundary (park or wilderness area)	△	mountain peak
⌐ - - - - - ⌐	tunnel	—	gate
(84)	interstate highway		body of water
(101)	U.S. highway		river or stream
(1) (530)	state highway		waterfall or cascade
2076	forest service road	—	dam or spillway
■	building	⊨	bridge
⛟	ranger station	) (	pass
		◄—	directional indicator

LAKE TAHOE AREA
From Highway 50 to Highway 80

LASSEN VOLCANIC NATIONAL PARK AREA
Highway 36 to Highway 44

MOUNT SHASTA AREA
Around Interstate 5

Acknowledgments

Heavy praise and thanks for the following hiking folks, friends, and family who gave love, kindness, and inspiration to me: Patricia Soares, Dionne Soares, Jake Soares, John Soares, Eric Soares, Camille Soares, Nancy Soares, Mozelle Berta, Les Berta, Rick Ramos, Derek Moss, Eric Pace, Peter Pace, Jayme Nicol, William F. Nicol II, Anne Nicol, William F. Nicol IV, Jon Palmer, and Bryan Buterbaugh.

The north face of Half Dome looms over Mirror Lake

11

Quaking aspens

Introduction

To an avid snowshoer, freshly fallen snowflakes spark a high-mountain hiking fever. Warning: Trudging in a slow dance rhythm over pure white heaven can be delightfully addictive, especially in the mighty mountains of Northern California. The best cure is to wait for winter and spring, head for these snow-clad slopes often, strap on snowshoes, and get to a special destination.

To be a snowshoer is to be part of a curious and unique breed. We're a mix of wanderlust and foolhardiness—the wild and artful peace-seekers of the world.

Snowshoeing is the safest and easiest way to travel over snow. Originating in Central Asia in 4000 B.C., snowshoeing is the earliest known means of snow travel. Aboriginal people made their exhausting journey to what is now North America via the Bering Strait only because of these "foot extenders" called snowshoes.

The recreational sport of snowshoeing has recently made a big comeback, with throngs of families, hikers, romancing couples, and vacationers appreciating this natural and modern-day method of gliding over snow. With a bit of planning, effort, and alertness, you can embrace the splendor of Northern California's bountiful backcountry even during the still of winter and the thrill of spring.

The rewards of experiencing communion with the natural and wild high country in winter and spring are numerous. The landscape looks strikingly different than it does in the dry summer. It is more serene and seems blessed with that thick coat of sound-absorbing snow, especially after the sky releases fresh powder. The gnats and mosquitoes are long gone, as are the crowds of folks.

Snowshoeing is almost as easy as walking. If you can get around with swim fins on, you're already a snowshoe connoisseur. With snowshoes, you can negotiate all but the steepest slopes. Time, energy, and weather can be limiting factors, but your imagination allows a plethora of snowshoeing options.

The intent of this book is to expand your hiking season via snowshoeing, share some special routes that are best seen snow-covered, and furnish a variety of snowshoe routes to fit your mood, energy level, and time allotment. In doing so, you'll have more fun, be more comfortable, more informed, more motivated, and above all, more touched.

WHY NORTHERN CALIFORNIA IS A PRIME PLACE FOR SNOWSHOEING

Opportunities galore. In Northern California, with elevations for snowshoeing ranging from 3,000 feet to 14,000 feet, the season can start as early as the Thanksgiving holiday and linger into May. Roughly two-thirds of the routes described in this book feature higher-elevation snowshoeing (6,000 feet and above). Forty of the routes are located in the Sierra Nevada, which generally feature a more desirable snow than other places. It's light and dry, like the weather. Typically, a lot of time passes between storms, giving the snowshoer more chances to enjoy snowshoeing in comfortable weather. The other routes are located in the Cascade Mountains, which receive more snow, often offering more days in the season for snowshoeing.

World-renowned destinations. Four routes in this book explore the flanks of mighty Mount Shasta, while five others offer awesome views of it. Five routes range within 4 miles of scenic Lassen Peak, and seven others feature fantastic views of it. Lake Tahoe is one of the top year-round vacation spots in the United States, and eight routes in this book are located within a few miles of this very large and beautiful high-mountain lake. Millions of people from around the world visit California's top outdoor tourist attraction, Yosemite National Park, each year. Fifteen routes described in this book are situated in this huge park or show views of parts of it.

Easy access and major highway access. All routes in this book offer good, paved roads to the trailhead and no-hassle parking. Only seven routes are more than 5 miles away from a major highway. Thirty routes are within about a 60-mile driving distance from Interstate 5 (or I-5), the most prominent and longest north–south freeway in the Pacific Northwest. All of the highways to snowshoe routes described in this book are promptly plowed, meaning there are only a few days out of the year when chains are required, other than an additional handful of mornings. Because Highway 395 (the gateway for nine routes in this book) is located in a desert zone just east of the Sierra Nevada, it seldom needs to be cleared of snow, even though it crosses near a series of snowshoe routes a bit higher up to the west at an elevation above 6,000 feet.

Many routes close to Sacramento, San Francisco, and Los Angeles. Five routes are within a 2-hour drive of Sacramento, and twenty-six are within about a 3-hour drive from the state's capital. Five routes are within a 3-hour drive of the San Francisco Bay Area, and twenty-six are within about a 4-hour drive.

Sixteen routes are within a 5-hour drive of the sprawling Los Angeles area. Forty routes are within the 6- to 7-hour range from Los Angeles.

Few pay sites. With the price of downhill skiing and snowboarding lift tickets continuing to rise ($20 to $50 per lift ticket), the free snowshoeing entry in most places in Northern California is a real bargain. In fact, only twenty routes in this book require a fee because they're within the boundaries of a national park or a Sno-Park.

Clear and easy-to-follow routes. Most of the routes in this book follow canyon bottoms along creeks or rivers, traipse around meadows, mount a peak mostly above tree line, or stay on snow-covered, wide roads—making snowshoeing in Northern California generally safe, comfortable, and hassle-free. Only a few routes require routefinding skills.

Breathtaking views. Because the snow line is often at or above tree line in snowshoe routes in Northern California, there are a lot of chances to gawk at unsurpassed, far-reaching views from panoramas atop ridges, passes, high slopes, and peaks. Thirty-two routes in this book feature fantastic, mind-blowing views, and several others offer good views as well. Check the handy Quick Trail Reference at the end of this book to find out which hikes offer great views.

Unique rocks and rock formations. The high backcountry of Northern California is a treasure trove of boulder outcrops, rocky cliffs, and other interesting geologic features. Twenty-one routes display major metamorphic, volcanic, or granitic rock showcases (see Quick Trail Reference).

Impressive trees. These would be the trees that often cause snowshoers to get out their cameras and put their film to good use. Nineteen routes in this book (see Trail Index) feature outstanding trees, whether they're huge (sequoias, incense cedars, sugar pines, and red firs), squat and picturesque with twisted trunks (Sierra junipers, Jeffrey pines, and whitebark pines), or picture perfect with handsome trunks (incense cedars, aspens, black cottonwoods, and ponderosa pines). Most other routes display outstanding tree qualities to lesser degrees. Northern California snowshoe country also features many other impressive trees, including Douglas fir, white fir, mountain hemlock, western white pine, and lodgepole pine. This variety is unsurpassed anywhere in the United States.

Good snow. Northern California ranks with Colorado for possessing the best snow in the west. This is mainly because there are more clear nights that lead to freezing temperatures than in places farther north. This "resets" the snow and reduces melt and mushiness.

Solitude. Virtually all of the snowshoe routes in this book promptly veer away from noisy traffic and any traces of civilization, and then stay that way for their entire length. Roughly a third of the routes are so unknown they're considered "best-kept secrets," and are mentioned as such in their chapters. This means you may have the entire area to yourself. Only a couple of routes allow snowmobiles, and that consideration is also mentioned in the route descriptions.

Convenient facilities. All but a few of the routes feature full-service facilities about a half hour's drive away, allowing you to spend the night in a hotel, get gas, and dine at a restaurant. For snowshoe routes 1–9, those towns include June Lake, Lee Vining, and Bridgeport. For snowshoe routes 10–19, towns include Oakhurst, Crane Flat, and El Portal. For snowshoe routes 20–33, there's the resort town of South Lake Tahoe, and for snowshoe routes 34–40, Tahoe City has full services available. For snowshoe routes 41–49, there's Susanville and Chester. For snowshoe routes 50–55, there's Burney, Shingletown, or Redding. For snowshoe routes 56–65, the towns of Mount Shasta, McCloud, and Weed offer full services.

Scenic drives to trailheads. It's almost as if the road builders had pleasing scenery and grand views in mind when they long ago planned the highways that now lead to snowshoe routes. If you're driving Highway 395, you're apt to see spacious Mono Lake and a staggering column of snow-capped peaks that exceed 11,000 feet in elevation. Highway 120 is the primary gateway to snowshoe routes 10–19, and you get to see Half Dome and other prominent rock domes from your car. Highway 88 offers a couple of high-mountain vista points, and you drive right by Silver Lake, Caples Lake, and Red Lake. Highway 50 features intimacy with the American River, Highway 89 is routed along the west shores of spacious Lake Tahoe, and Highway 80 passes near Donner Lake and Donner Pass. Highways 36, 44, and 89 offer many views of Lassen Peak, and I-5 for miles and miles showcases Lassen Peak, Mount Shasta, Castle Crags, the Sacramento River, Shasta Lake, the Klamath Mountains, and the Yolla Bollys.

SNOWSHOES

Several state-of-the-art snowshoe types are available at outdoor supply stores, just be sure to get a pair with ice spikes called crampons or cleats under the forefoot and heel plates. There are snowshoes for virtually every type of snow, but folks almost always settle for one pair. I suggest a middle-of-the-road pair for most snow conditions. They won't be the best choice for 2 feet of powder or total ice, but then again, in those snow conditions it may be best to choose another time to go snowshoeing. Large snowshoes are best for deep powder while short shoes are best suited for icy snow. Most folks weighing less than 180 pounds will be satisfied with snowshoes in the 8-by-25-inch range or smaller. Larger snowshoers or those carrying heavy packs should probably go

Snow bridge and quaking aspens

for shoes in the 9-by-30-inch category. Big guys with very heavy packs can go up to a 9-by-36-inch shoe. Consider renting a few times to help decide which size and type is best for you. The good news is that snowshoes are far more efficient, lighter, and easier to use these days. Ski poles give you a good upper body workout and keep you more stable. Poles also come in handy when backing up or turning around. You may not need them for mostly flat routes.

CLOTHING AND WARMTH

The key is to wear and/or pack layers of synthetic clothing (avoid cotton because it doesn't dry out fast enough) from outdoor supply stores. With layering, you can easily add clothing when you cool down from sweating or when winds kick up, or take off garments when you heat up from climbing.

From the skin out, begin with synthetic-based long johns (for upper and lower body). They form an important, insulating layer against your skin, but also wick moisture away from your body. Then put on a fleece sweater and fleece pants and stuff a thicker fleece jacket in your pack. For wind, rain, and snow protection, put on or take a waterproof Gore-Tex parka (with waterproof hood) and nylon shell pants. All clothes should be light and loose fitting.

It's preferred to use a pair of thin, synthetic socks, then put thick fleece-type socks over them, then carry an extra pair in your pack. Mitts are a must—they keep your hands warmer than gloves. If you go with gloves, get them a

17

size larger than your hands. Tight gloves inhibit circulation and don't trap warm air as well. It's ideal to go with mitts made of a synthetic material that is waterproof on the outside. Most of your heat is lost through the head, so a good cap made of synthetic material that at least covers the ears and part of the neck is important. Keeping your feet warm and dry is crucial. Boots must be good-fitting, comfortable, and sturdy enough to support the foot when they're slid into snowshoes. Winter boots are better, but summer boots can be worn. Check with your local backcountry retailer for the best water-protection product for your type of boot. Gaiters don't have to be worn if your nylon pants are long enough to cover the top half of your boots.

Staying dry in snow country is the key and also a big challenge. You can get wet from slipping or dropping clothes onto the snow as well as from sweating. Snow manages to sneak inside your boots and slowly melt. Being cold deprives you of your ability to use good judgment and make good decisions.

OTHER ESSENTIAL GEAR

Here's a handy list of important stuff that must be taken along, with most of it always staying in your pack.

The Ten Essentials

1. **Extra clothing.** There should be enough layers stashed in your pack to keep you warm enough if you had to suddenly stay the night in the backcountry. Remember, when you stop moving you get cold right away.
2. **Water and extra food.** Even in warm weather perishable foods stay fresh in snow country. Bring enough food so you have leftovers.
3. **Sunglasses.** Without them, you could be squinting in pain, all teary-eyed, especially in sunlit snow that reflects back onto your face. Sunburn of the eyes (snow blindness) can leave you helpless and immobile. Use sunglasses that filter out at least 90 percent of the UVA/UVB rays.
4. **Multitool knife.** From first aid to whittling kindling, a knife can come in handy, especially in emergencies.
5. **First-aid kit.** Include adhesive and gauze bandages, antacids, and pain-relief medicine. Ibuprofen tends to control inflammation the best.
6. **Fire starter.** You'll find it's a necessity when trying to start a fire in snow country, where everything is wet.
7. **Matches.** Keep them in waterproof containers and go with high-quality stick matches.
8. **Flashlight.** Change batteries before they get weak, and always click the flashlight on to see if it works. A flashlight can allow you to make out the route or set up emergency camp in the dark.

9. **Map.** Carry a topo map and know how to read it.

10. **Compass.** Carry a compass and know how to use it.

Along with these ten items, I recommend the following additions:

Sunblock. Applying a high-powered sunblock is the first thing you should do when you park at the trailhead. Then stick it back in your pack. Spending spring days in the sunlit snow especially requires sunblock.

Watch. Knowing the time can help you make decisions about whether to turn back or go a bit farther.

Optional items include rope and/or string, toilet paper, this book, lip balm, duct tape, a Mylar blanket, film and camera, binoculars, a whistle, clothespins, keys, and money.

CONDITIONS

Weather. High-country weather during snowshoe season can range from mellow and comfortable to extreme. Gusty, bone-chilling north winds or an incessant onslaught of snow adds more risk while slowing you down. For snowshoeing, you get most of the news you need from the weather report. Always obtain the very latest report for the area that you're visiting. Log on to *www.weather.com*, then type in the nearest town to your snowshoe destination in the "local weather" section on the top left portion of the screen. You will receive instant, updated, and detailed weather information. Keep in mind that weather forecasts change and are amended frequently, especially in the high country and during snowshoeing season. In the final analysis, let your eyes be your guide when you get there. If the weather is too inclement, bag it. There will always be another chance.

Chains. Keep chains in the trunk, and be sure to try them on in the comfort of your driveway first to make sure you can successfully get them on in more challenging conditions. If chains are required over large stretches of highway, that's a sign the new snow may be too deep for easy snowshoeing. Consider going some other time. Get the latest road conditions across Northern California's highways by calling the Caltrans road condition phone number at 1-800-427-7623.

Avalanches. Avalanches start with unstable snow—snow that isn't bonded to the hillside. The most avalanche-prone areas include slopes between 30 and 45 degrees, treeless slopes, gullies, north-facing slopes in winter, south-facing slopes in spring, and convex (bulging outward) slopes. As much as possible, avoid these areas, especially during periods of instability. (Call the information source ahead of time to find out the latest conditions before you leave.) If you're in a suspect avalanche spot, proceed quickly, one at a time. It's safer to follow ridges wherever possible.

Silver Lake

Visible clues to avalanche danger are wind, sticky snow, evidence of recent avalanches, broken limbs and/or snow plastered on the uphill side of trees, rime ice on trees, and hollow "whomping" sounds underfoot. A good book on the subject is *The ABCs of Avalanche Safety,* second edition, by Ed LaChapelle (Mountaineers Books, 1985).

Cornices. As impressive of a natural wonder as an avalanche, a cornice is an overhanging mass of snow at the crest of a ridge formed where prevailing winds drift snowfall leeward over the edge. Eventually and without warning, cornices will break off and plunge to the slope below. Avoid ridge edges, and for that matter, avoid stepping on edges of snow over streams, for although they're not cornices, they may break off from the impact and cause your leg to lurch downward.

ROUTEFINDING

Finding your way over snow-covered terrain is an important backcountry skill that's well worth your time to learn how to do. In most cases, there are no signs, no trails, and no people around to help you get oriented. Unless you're following a marked trail or someone else's prelaid tracks, you must remember landmarks and study backcountry features closely. You must comprehend the topo map in your pack that pertains to the place you're visiting. Here are some important principles to follow:

1. If in doubt deep in the backcountry, be prepared to retrace your tracks until you get reoriented.
2. Always leave a written, detailed description of your route with somebody at home.
3. Always study your route meticulously before leaving home.
4. Always carry a compass and a topo map of the area, and know how to read them.
5. Always keep your party together along the route.
6. Chances are that entering thickets of chaparral or picking and choosing your way among huge rock outcrops are not the right routes.
7. Keep in mind it's harder to orient on cloud-socked days.

TYPES OF SNOW

The wide variety of snow types can affect comfort and safety during your snow-shoe outing. By calling ahead to the governing agency for the region, you can find out the type of snow that presently exists to help you make better decisions, such as whether to go, to abbreviate the trip, to change snowshoes, etc.

Corn snow. Partial melting during warm spring days followed by solid freezing at night produces large, rounded grains known as corn snow. Seldom formed in winter, corn snow makes for effortless snowshoeing.

Packed powder. This is what you get if it's been a couple of days or more since the last snowfall. Packed powder (settled snow) provides good stability and usually good footing. In time, it resettles and refreezes so much that it can become ice snow.

Deep powder. Often sticking to your boots unless it's a very dry powder from a very cold snow (below 28 degrees or so), this phenomenon occurs during or just after a heavy snowfall. It's not safe, in particular because you can pull or fatigue your leg muscles from the repeated lifting to awkward heights that this snow requires.

Powder on packed powder. A desirable snowshoe surface, this condition occurs when a few inches or less of new snow has fallen on settled snow.

Snow crust. When daytime temperatures completely melt the upper layer of snow crystals, the resulting sheet of water may freeze at night to form a meltwater crust. Winds also form snow crusts, through blowing and breaking up surface crystals, which then resettle more compactly. Snow crust is a form of packed powder that causes a crunching sound with each step and furnishes good footing throughout most of a typical day.

Ice snow. This forms as packed snow gets old, yet still freezes at night. You'll need to dig your snowshoe cleats firmly into this hard and slippery surface to avoid falling. This condition is more pronounced during cold mornings and late afternoons when packed snow, which is mostly water, refreezes.

Rotten snow. Meltwater coursing through the snowpack in spring carves out large cavities hidden beneath the surface. Eventually, the snow above these cavities collapses, sometimes prematurely when a hiker steps on them in late spring or early summer.

Suncups. These scalloped snow surfaces are created by uneven heating and melting. Suncups tend to form during the clear, warm days that are typical of spring as dry air moves over a snowfield where surface irregularities have begun forming. The hollows diminish faster than the raised areas, approaching 3 feet in depth, making for tedious travel.

Watermelon snow. Portions of snowbanks may be stained a bright watermelon pink from mid-spring into summer. Algae growing in the snow as it melts cause the color. These minute plant organisms are actually green, but they secrete the pink, gelatinous coating around themselves, probably for solar radiation protection.

WHAT TO LOOK FOR WHILE SNOWSHOEING

Things in the backcountry that tend to get overlooked in the warm months suddenly shine when there's snow. Animal tracks seem more frequent and conspicuous when their impressions are temporarily molded in the snow. Look for the footprints of weasels, snow rabbits, deer, and coyotes. The once cheerfully green grasses of the meadow expose themselves in melted margins of the field. Here, next to the snow, they cling to the soggy ground as stringy, shreddy, gray-brown laces. The leaves and needles that were formerly yellow and green, full and lush, are now crispy brown, wrinkled and rotting in the snow. Areas labeled as mundane in the summer, such as roads, man-made clearings, clutter, and debris, get a second chance to look scenic when blanketed with snow.

Snowshoe sights vary with the weather and snow conditions. Old snow in the forest is dappled with dark dust, as it begins to pick up dirt and debris like an unswept floor. Old snow on a bright day seems harsh. Old snow makes a different sound from the impact of snowshoes than fresh snow does. If you're snowshoeing soon after a snowstorm, the conifer boughs are beautifully burdened by fluffy white powder. Each evergreen conifer, large or small, is a Christmas-tree-like specimen. New snow also clings to the limbs of the deciduous trees and shrubs, but in much smaller proportions. Aspen, cottonwood, and willow limbs are dusted with pencil-thin snow, which melts cleanly and quickly, shining in the midday sun. Note how the conifer boughs gradually shed their snow by a combination of melting and falling. White fir and red fir boughs hold the snow more perfectly upright, while lodgepole, Jeffrey, and ponderosa pine boughs droop and hang more with snow. Incense cedars seem to hold snow as thin, wide sheets. Big, flat-topped boulders weighing 100 pounds or more form snow pillows after a snowstorm. They appear like firm pillows if just a few inches of snow fell, and more like big fluffy throw pillows if a lot of snow recently collected on the boulders. The snow pillows take center stage in a stream, and they're decorative as snow pillow stumps in meadows. Icicles in an array of odd shapes and sizes appear, especially in shaded spots after hard freezes where there's extra moisture on hard objects such as roots, rocks, and branches.

Birds are more discreet amid the wintry snow. Even a minor act such as a bird departing from a low limb seems noisy and pleasantly distracting, especially when snow drops from the swaying limb. Birds seem to congregate in bigger, tighter flocks in snow country. You're more apt to see them in the early morning or late afternoon on sunny days, and just before or just after a storm on cloudy days.

Cloudscapes mingle amiably with snow in the backcountry. It's especially dramatic in the high, exposed open areas above tree line. The pure white can be blinding and harsh when it's high and bright overcast, or soft and heavenly when it's low overcast or when shadows creep in.

Trees and shrubs politely beckon your attention more in snowshoe country. In a forest, they attract your attention as a collective unit. In exposed areas, each tree competes for your gaze as specimens. One evergreen tree, the incense cedar, and a deciduous shrub, the willow, are very common throughout Northern California high country, and look their best during snowshoe season.

Incense cedar. This native conifer spreads its welcoming arms throughout high- and low-mountain forests in Northern California, and it is often a familiar ally on snowshoe treks. When the wild wind stirs the forest, the sound it makes against incense cedars is not like a whistle, it's more like a tenor chant. Graceful with its bright green sprays of evergreen foliage, and elegant with its deeply furrowed, thick yet soft, reddish bark, this noble giant among trees can breathe cheer and inspiration into a dreary winter day.

Incense cedar *(calocedrus decurrens)* is the one conifer that rarely dominates but embellishes both black oak woodland and high mountain forests with its majestic, pyramidal form. From a distance, the entire tree looks like an upside-down, long, flowing beard.

Long ago, famous mountaineer John Muir often sought shelter from a storm, along with stormbound birds, beneath the aromatic boughs of incense

Bunny Flat and Mount Shasta

cedars because the scaly, fernlike plumes shed rain and snow like a thatched roof. Sierra Indians built huts called *oochums* from their durable, fibrous bark. Well-adapted to the western climate, incense cedars can live more than 700 years and reach heights of 150 feet. Aphids, mistletoe, and several little-known fungi can attack the foliage and trunk, but they usually do little damage.

Willows. You've seen more of the cheery, native willow shrubs thriving as thickets, drifts, and colonies along meadows, streams, and lakes than any other shrub by far. But because these high-country regions usually feature other visual standouts, such as snow-capped mountainous views or cascades, the common willow plays second fiddle, even though it usually looks clean, informal, and presentable.

Willow shrubs *(salix species)* are the last deciduous bushes to lose their leaves in late autumn and they are the harbingers of spring by being the first to leaf out while the snow often still stands.

The high-elevation native willow shrubs in particular are in their visual prime in winter when out of leaf, boldly showing off their flashy orange or lemon yellow clumps of slim stems. This eye-catching scene becomes more impressive when shreds of snow, beads of ice, or water droplets cling to the bare switches, making them even more shiny.

Sometimes during early snowshoe season, the lance-shaped leaves are still turning color when all other deciduous trees and shrubs have shed their leaves. It's a treat to discover the yellow to orange leaves lying in the snow, while others still hang on the limbs. Late in the snowshoe season, the leaf and flower buds swell to proportions that appear abnormal, seemingly ready to burst like popcorn. The fuzzy, flowery catkins typically emerging in late winter or early spring are always uniquely decorative and sometimes silvery or yellow in their cast.

Fast-growing and carefree, willow shrubs feature elegant foliage and graceful form, and they're useful to boot. Willow bark is used by herbalists as a substitute for aspirin. The bendable wood has long been used by Native Americans in making durable baskets and poles for teepees. Many small birds of Northern California, especially the white-crowned sparrow, seek cover in the shrub willows.

Willows are sun worshippers, naturalizing primarily in open spots, often with southwestern exposure. Although typically short-lived (10 to 20 years), willow shrubs function as natural erosion control on lake and pond edges, stream banks, and moist slopes.

CONIFERS

Way back in the days before humans came along, when only a few plant types had evolved, conifers took center stage. These days people are fascinated with these cone-bearing, narrow-leaved, needled evergreen trees. Merely mention an enchanted forest and the first thing that pops to mind are pines and firs, and maybe some sequoias, junipers, and cedars. Mention the Pacific Northwest to a foreigner and the first thing that's bound to come to mind is a conifer.

In the Northern California native high-country where snowshoeing takes place, conifers are by far the most prominent wild plants, and also the most highly admired. They create a charming note of cherished green that sets off or frames meadows and skylines. When snowshoeing, conifers produce the bulk of the green that mingles with the white of snow.

If you're snowshoeing soon after snowfall, note that Douglas firs, white firs, red firs, and incense cedars have stiff boughs, and typically hold snow longer than pines, sequoias, junipers, and hemlocks. Pines and junipers tend to congregate in more sun-exposed, open areas, and therefore snow melts beneath them faster than beneath other Northern California conifers. Conversely, white firs and red firs tend to colonize in dense forests along more protected east- and/or north-facing slopes, and therefore snow lingers on the ground the longest time beneath them. You'll also find the most big boulders nestled among

Jeffrey pines and ponderosa pines, and the fewest boulders next to white firs and red firs. Jeffrey pines and ponderosa pines are hard to tell apart, partly because they're the only high-country conifers with needles in bunches of three. Both feature checkerboard-like bark that is fragrant if you sniff it from up close, especially when the sun has been shining on it. The best way to discern Jeffrey pine from ponderosa pine is by the cones. Grab a cone and squeeze it. If it hurts from sharpness, it's a ponderosa pine. Remember—it's "prickly" ponderosa and "gentle" Jeffrey. These two pines tend to grow in lean soils lacking fertility and often full of rocks.

At low snow line, Douglas firs and incense cedars dominate in developed soils, usually ones covered in a deep litter of leaves, needles, twigs, and cones. They tend to thrive with the protection of being in a deep forest, benefiting from extra shade refuge while young. Douglas firs are the most abundant conifers in Northern California, followed by ponderosa pines, Jeffrey pines, and white firs.

Fallen Leaf Lake and Mount Tallac

Not a true fir, Douglas fir often mingles with white fir and to a lesser extent red fir, the two true firs of Northern California. Now the most common conifers in Lassen National Forest since fire suppression, white and red firs often occupy pure stands along east- and north-facing slopes. All the above-mentioned conifers are found throughout snow country in Northern California in abundance. A handful of other conifers are occasionally interspersed throughout the high country, including mountain hemlocks, lodgepole pines, whitebark pines, sugar pines (with their foot-long cones), and western white pines.

The giant sequoias are limited to a few groves near and in Yosemite National Park. Sierra junipers are limited to high country in the Sierra Nevada, including the Lake Tahoe area. Western junipers are basically limited to Lassen National Forest and Lassen Park high country.

The two-needled lodgepole pines form the boundary of high mountain lakes and meadows. Formerly known as tamaracks, they dominate along meadow and lake edges in the high country. Whitebark pines (five needles to a bunch) join Jeffrey pines atop high ridges and mountains. Because of fierce winds, no shade, and huge snow accumulations in these places, these conifers grow more shrublike than treelike.

Conifers are typically thought of as being green, but some of Northern California's conifers have needles that are just as gray as green. They include mountain hemlock, sequoia, juniper, gray pine, and knobcone pine.

CRASH COURSE ON TAKING GREAT PHOTOS IN THE SNOW

The keys to better shots out in the snow-covered hinterlands are patience, understanding your camera, knowing what makes a good photo, and being in the right place at the right time.

Your camera. Of course, having a good camera helps. A camera that can be focused manually and has knobs and/or switches for manually changing f-stops and shutter speeds goes a long way toward improved photos. Better yet, get a telezoom camera that goes from wide angle all the way to telephoto with a simple turn of the lens dial. This lets you compose the best possible photo by zooming in or out while viewing the scene.

The art of taking great shots in the snow. If you think you've come to a spot where there's a great photo opportunity, then chances are you're at the right place at the right time. Or perhaps the right time might be "more right" later. Take photos at that moment, do some more snowshoeing and/or picnicking, and try to check the spot again before heading back to see if light conditions improved. The main thing is to capitalize on the moment when you sense you're at a good spot. This means taking several shots with different meter readings, verticals and horizontals, wide angles versus telezooms, and shots from different spots. The following tips will help you take great photos on your snowshoeing excursions:

1. Bracket your shots. This means taking two or three photos of the same scene, altering the exposure by half to a full stop (aperture click) or the shutter speed one full click, after metering with your light meter. This way, you should ideally get one photo slightly underexposed, another slightly overexposed, and still another according to your meter. You can't always trust your meter.

2. Be patient, think clearly and thoroughly, be confident and artful.

3. Let your heart rate slow down from the snowshoeing exertion, drink some water, and put on some layers of warm clothes.

4. If the sun is about to dip behind major cloud cover for a long while, then proactively get a few shots beforehand. The sun shining on your subject as well as the background provides more even lighting, more detail, more highlights, and more shadows—all desirable attributes in a good photo.

5. Walk around the area, sampling photo candidates through your viewfinder. Refuse to settle for the first thing you see, for there's likely to be a better shot in a spot perhaps a few feet away.

6. Squat down, lean over, stand on something—one of these acts is bound to reveal an improved composition through the viewfinder.

7. Before clicking off a shot, make sure your camera isn't tilted. In most cases, it should be level and straight, especially for photos that include lakes and skylines.

8. Before clicking the shot, double-check the four corners in the frame to make sure there's nothing obtrusive, stupid-looking, or distracting in the frame. If there is something in one or more corners and you want it out, move the camera away, move up a bit, or zoom in a bit until the object completely disappears.

9. In most cases, the primary subject should be anywhere from slightly to considerably off center.

10. Avoid bright rocks or snags in the foreground; or pour water from a nearby creek or lake over them to create a darkened effect and remove the glare.

11. Avoid clutter, especially in the foreground. This includes powerlines, roads, litter or other signs of civilization, branches, or indistinct objects such as bushes.

12. Always check to determine if a vertical shot might be better. This may especially be the case for vertical subjects such as waterfalls, tall mountains, and standing humans.

13. When looking for a good shot, and also when scanning in the viewfinder, there are a lot of things to look for. This includes graceful lines and shapes, unique boulders, moving water with white in it, totally still water with unique specimens (usually mountains) reflecting in it, fall colors, cloudscapes (especially streaky cirrus and puffy cumulus clouds), trees casting shadows in the foreground, colorful rocks (maybe with lichens), branch patterns (such as willows in winter), and exposed ground next to snow.

14. Sometimes it's best if possible to make a short climb to look down on a subject. It's important to know before taking off on your snowshoe outing that higher-quality shots are usually found above timberline. Take a camera with plenty of film for sure if you're going above timberline because you'll get more open and improved views.

Good timing. The days are short during snowshoe season, and the sun moves from east to west from the south, not directly overhead like in mid-summer. This means there's a much shorter window of opportunity for good photos, for in the mountains during the short days, there's too much shadow in the early morning and late afternoon. Therefore, the best times for taking photos in the snow during winter and early spring are usually from 9 A.M. to noon and from 2 P.M. to 4:30 P.M. If the sun is at least mostly out, this will likely get you more intense highlights and more dramatic shadows. Plan ahead so that your anticipated primary subjects are in full light. This means showing from the west in the morning and showing from the east in the late afternoon. Note that it's also more likely to be cloudy in the early morning than in the mid-afternoon in the winter.

People in snow shots. For snapshots in snow country with friends or family smiling close-up for the camera, you're on your own. But snow country photos with people discriminately modeling can result in a quality nature photo that doubles as a photo of your friend(s) or family member(s). The key to successful shots of this type is for the subjects to belong to the scene. They should look comfortable, and it's best for the subjects not to look directly at the camera. Instead, they should have their backs turned or be turned slightly to the side so you can see hair, an ear, a cheek, and an eye. In most cases, people should be at least 15 feet away in a nature shot and can be up to as far as 40 yards away, as long as you can still tell a person is there. It's a good idea to count to three, then take the shot. It's also good to instruct your subjects on where to put their hands, feet, and heads. Generally, you want them positioned at the side of the frame, or near the bottom or top, but not in the middle. In most cases, you want them looking into the scene, not away from the picture. Avoid bright white shirts or clothing that advertises a brand name.

Close-up photos. Focus sharply on the main subject, whether it's a mushroom, a flower, an icicle, a swollen willow branch, a snow-covered log, a boulder, etc. If someone is with you, have them place an item with big, easy-to-read print in the exact spot where the main subject is. Be sure to take your meter reading and form your composition first. Focus until the print is clear, have your helper gently move the item away, and then take the shot. The subject looks sharper and the frame matter in the background looks more artistic when only the subject is in focus and the secondary elements in the photo become less focused the farther away they are from the sharply focused, primary subject. To achieve this, open your f-stop to somewhere around f-4 or f-5.6. It's important to note that the lower the f-stop number, the less that is in focus, which is desirable most of the time in close-up nature photography. A lower number (wide open, such as 2.8 or lower, is too narrow of a focus, and sometimes there is not enough of the subject in focus) allows a faster shutter speed. With any close-up photography featuring subject matter that may move in the wind, a fast shutter speed helps tremendously. It's important to know that fast shutter speeds generally mean sharper photos of any kind. If you're shooting flowers or grass or any other subject matter that is blowing in the wind, keep aiming the camera steady until the wind abates, then click away. A good deal of close-up photography can be done on overcast days.

Depth of field. When you want something in the foreground and infinity to be in focus, you can try turning the focus dial about one quarter of an inch from total infinity at the far end of where the dial stops. And, turn the f-stop to a high number such as f-11, f-16, or f-22. The higher the f-stop number on the aperture, the more that is in focus. Most manual cameras have a focus chart on the camera that indicates how much is in focus based on where the focus dial is and what f-stop it's switched to. For long-distance shots from 30 feet to infinity, focus all the way to the far end of the focus dial on infinity. Since depth of field is not crucial in this situation, shoot with a faster shutter speed and a lower f-stop number. This helps make the shot sharper. If light and extra depth of field are not an issue, set the f-stop at f-5.6 or f-8, then meter to determine the shutter speed.

Shutter speed. Shooting at slower than $\frac{1}{60}$ of a second generally means a tripod should be used. You can go tripodless down to $\frac{1}{30}$ of a second shutter speed or perhaps a bit slower by doing the following: slow your heart rate by resting first, then breathing deeply and slowly; brace your elbows; lean against something solid; wait until wind gusts cease. Of course, these four steps should be used all the time and can also improve sharpness in fast-speed shots.

For creamy rapids and cascades, use a tripod at $\frac{1}{8}$ of a second or slower.

Thunder Mountain and Caples Lake

Or, find a level rock etc., rest the camera level on piled or folded clothing, and then shoot without holding the camera.

Film speed. Even in snow, light conditions can vary or be low lit. Unless you pack a tripod, which most people don't when they're snowshoeing or hiking, it's best to carry high-speed films such as ASA 400. This allows you more depth of field when you want it, or a faster shutter speed if you need it. The difference between an ASA 400 film speed and an ASA 64 film speed is this: With the same f-stop setting, you can shoot ASA 400 at a shutter speed of $\frac{1}{250}$ of a second compared with being stuck with a shutter speed of $\frac{1}{30}$ of a second when using ASA 64.

Special light conditions. Use a polarizing filter in most situations when there is blue sky. This darkens the sky and reduces glare, but keeps the clouds bright. Keep in mind, using a polarizing filter reduces the light entering your camera by up to two full f-stops. All the more reason to use a higher-speed film, such as ASA 400. Be sure to take off your polarizing filter for anything but subject matter involving blue sky or blue lakes. Be sure to bracket with your shots. (See the section above on artistic shots, tip number 1.)

For bright, hazy, and/or overcast sky, use as little sky in your frame as possible. Light meter off everything but the sky. With a sun and cloud mix, compose your shot, then wait until the sun comes out fully from behind the clouds before shooting (meter first, then shoot). Avoid shooting directly into the sun, which causes loss of detail and glare.

Metering for snow. Try metering on everything but the snow, then shoot. Or, meter on just the snow, then open up two to three f-stops, and then shoot. Or, meter off the whole scene, open up one f-stop, and then shoot.

WILDERNESS ETHICS

Trudging over snow is already lower impact than stepping on and therefore gradually compacting bare ground. It's also generally quieter than crunching on twigs, leaves, and stones.

Going to the wilderness is granted via special invitation from nature. We should show our appreciation by taking nothing but photographs and leaving only footprints.

Trail etiquette. Yield the right of way to cross-country skiers and snowmobilers. Avoid snowshoeing on existing cross-country ski tracks. This lets skiers reuse their tracks on the return trip, and allows others to have a smooth groove to ski in. Keep pets (if allowed) and their by-products under control.

Resist the temptation to shortcut up and down switchbacks when snow is sparse. This destroys trailside plant life and accelerates trail erosion. Your philosophy should be that of minimum impact, which means striving to leave no trace of your visit.

Camping. Minimum-impact philosophy also applies to campsites. Select a site at least 100 feet away from lakes, streams, and rivers so that you won't disturb waterside plants or pollute the water. However, if the only site you find is an established site less than 100 feet from the water, then use it carefully. Whenever possible, use an existing site in the forest or one that's far from the water. Finally, put a plastic tarp under your tent to protect yourself from rainwater. Never dig ditches.

Fires. The minimum-impact hiker doesn't need a fire. Burning wood removes organic material from the ecosystem, contributes to air pollution, and scares away animal life. Bring enough clothes to ensure night warmth. If you must have a hot meal, bring a gas stove; however, you can enjoy a wide variety of foods that don't require cooking. If you insist on having a fire, do so only in or near heavily wooded areas, make it a small fire, and use only down deadwood in an established campfire ring.

Shasta Lake and Bridge Bay

Washing. Detergents and food particles harm water life and can alter water chemistry, so wash yourself and your dishes far from lakes and streams. Carry water off to the woods or a bare rock for washing, and use biodegradable soaps available from outdoor stores or nothing.

Sanitation. Defecate in a shallow hole 6 to 10 inches deep, preferably in forest duff where the covered feces will quickly decompose. Be sure your spot is at least 200 feet from water and well away from trails and campsites. You needn't be so careful with urine because it's sterile. But do stay away from water sources, and don't pee all over any single plant. Spread it around and let it provide the soil with valuable nitrogen.

Garbage. Pack it all out, including any you find that's not yours.

Hiker courtesy. Your goal is to be as unnoticeable and unobtrusive as possible. Choose subdued colors such as gray, green, and brown for your clothing and equipment. Travel only in small groups. Set up an inconspicuous camp. Talk in quiet tones.

HOW TO USE THIS BOOK

This guidebook features carefully chosen routes to suit all abilities and moods, with a blend of "cakewalks" and "buttkickers," family walks, winter backpack trips, all-day hikes, and half-day hikes. Choose from an array of routes in or near Yosemite National Park, Lake Tahoe, Lassen Park, and Mount Shasta. Keep this book in the glove compartment of your vehicle during the drive for easy access, then take it with you so you can read excerpts of your route along the way.

Each route description is broken into four basic parts: a hike summary heads each chapter and is followed by the trip's highlights, directions to the trailhead, and finally a guide to the route, including landmarks and view descriptions. It's a good idea to read the entire route description before choosing a hike. You'll find out where the uphills, downhills, clearings, forests, rock outcrops, and ridge tops are located. You'll also find information on identification of the prominent native trees to help boost your tree knowledge and appreciation.

The hike summaries give you the following basic information about trip length and difficulty, elevation, maps, and who to call for more information.

Total Distance. This is the total round-trip distance for the hike, unless otherwise specified. Note that if you're short on energy or time, you don't have to do the entire route in order to have a great trip. Read the guide section (main body of each chapter text) for distances to ideal turnaround points, such as viewpoints, meadows, creeks, and lakes. Note that extra hiking may need to be factored in if the snow line is lower than the described parking area. For most hikes in this book, however, you should be able to reach the described parking area most of the time.

Hiking time. This is a subjective indicator that allows the average snowshoer ample time for eating, taking photos, removing or putting on clothing, book or map reading, and resting. Allow plenty of time to return safely to your car way before it gets dark, which is as early as 5 P.M. in the winter. Keep in mind that snowshoeing takes at least 50 percent more time than hiking a trail to get to the same destination.

Difficulty. The terms *easy, moderate,* and *strenuous* are subjective, factoring in distance, elevation gains and losses, and trail conditions. Easy could seem moderate to a nonhiker, while strenuous could seem moderate to a distance runner. Other factors can make hikes seem difficult, such as heavy winds, flying snow, deep snow, soreness, or being thirsty or hungry. Some hikes rated strenuous might be easy for the first couple of miles, and therefore might make an ideal short hike for those wanting an easier trip. Many hikes use two of these terms (for example, moderate to strenuous) to better describe the difficulty factor. The term *strenuous* can also mean extra routefinding, navigation, and avalanche danger.

Elevation gain. This is the accumulated total amount of climbing for the route, round trip. Downhills on the way out that have to be climbed on the way back are counted.

High point. This is the elevation of the highest point along the route, not necessarily the end point.

Maps. So lightweight yet so important, reading maps keeps you safer and enhances enjoyment during your trip. Topo maps are especially meaningful during winter, when snow conceals trails. By examining topo maps and reading the chapter text describing the hike, you can orient yourself and stay on course. Note that the maps in this book are meant as locator maps to help you visualize the route, show the major place names, and assist you in spotting the route on a topo map. I indicate which U.S. Geological Survey (USGS) topo map is needed for each route, and maps can be bought at most engineering supply stores and outdoor supply stores. Acquire and print topo maps over the Web at *www.topozone.com*. Topo maps are a cinch to decipher by studying the legend on each map. For getting to your destination, take along a California highway map or state atlas or U.S. Forest Service maps.

Information. This is the governing agency with jurisdiction over the area that includes the hike. Phone numbers are listed in a special appendix at the end of the book. You may have to leave a message on a machine, so call well in advance. Call to ask about permits, user fees, weather, snow and avalanche conditions, and road conditions.

A NOTE ABOUT SAFETY

Safety is an important concern in all outdoor activities. No guidebook can alert you to every hazard or anticipate the limitations of every reader. Therefore, the descriptions of roads, trails, routes, and natural features in this book are not representations that a particular place or excursion will be safe for your party. When you follow any of the routes described in this book, you assume responsibility for your own safety. Under normal conditions, such excursions require the usual attention to traffic, road and trail conditions, weather, terrain, the capabilities of your party, and other factors. Keeping informed on current conditions and exercising common sense are the keys to a safe, enjoyable outing.

The Mountaineers Books

Rabbitbrush, Twin Lake, and Crater Crest

EASTERN SIERRA NEVADA

Highway 395 from Tioga Pass Area to Sonora Pass

--*1*--

Minaret Vista and San Joaquin Ridge

Total distance: Up to 9.4 miles; 4.8 miles round trip for Deadman Pass
Hiking time: 6–9 hours
Difficulty: Moderate to strenuous
Elevation gain: 2,600 feet
High point: 11,387 feet
Map: USGS Mammoth Mountain
Information: Ansel Adams Wilderness

Roam the curving spine of the San Joaquin Ridge, which is steeped in breath-taking high-mountain scenery where the eye can see for miles and miles in all directions. From the get go and throughout, the views of Mount Clyde, Mount Ritter, and Banner Peak to the west are superb, and by the time you reach the top of Two Teats, a final panorama unfolds that includes Mono Lake to the northeast and prominent Yosemite National Park peaks.

Most folks are satisfied to get well away from the crowds, bag Deadman Pass, and head back with a batch of spectacular photos. The rough and bumpy dirt road that doubles as a hiking path after the snow melts makes for an ideal snowshoe route in winter. The hike is shadeless and therefore sometimes windy, so bring plenty of water, a windbreaker, sunblock, sunglasses, and hat. Check ahead for avalanche danger if you're snowshoeing beyond Deadman Pass to Two Teats. The wide route to Deadman Pass is obvious, and it's discernible even after a dumping of fresh snow or during a light snowstorm. Because of the extra-high elevation at the starting point, this is a route that often can be snowshoed into April and May, even if you have to lug your snowshoes to the snow line.

To get there, turn west on Road 203 at Mammoth Junction from Highway 395. Drive about 3 miles through the town of Mammoth Lakes, then go right at the sign indicating Devils Postpile. Continue 5.5 miles, climbing on paved road and following signs for Minaret Vista. Park for free in the large lot near the interpretive signs and the bathroom, which fronts the unsigned trailhead.

A slim path, usually detected from the snowshoe and cross-country ski tracks, leads north a hundred yards or so, connecting with the snow-covered old dirt road, where you bear left on it. After a 0.5-mile climb, reach a flat featuring scattered young lodgepole pines. Stroll west on it a few paces for fantastic views of the Minarets, which are mainly Mount Clyde, Mount Ritter,

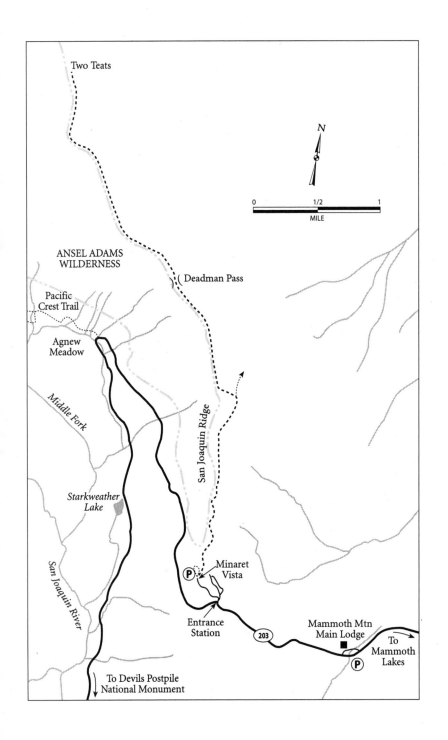

and Banner Peak. Their glaciers are gleaming white in the morning, converting gradually to dull gray by late afternoon.

At 0.8 mile, look behind you for sensational views of Mammoth Mountain, Laurel Mountain, and 12,268-foot-tall Mount Morrison, from west to east. Continue your steady ascent past red firs, whitebark pines, lodgepole pines, and mountain hemlocks over snow covering loose and crumbly pumice, remnants of the region's hot volcanic history. The San Joaquin Ridge is part of the Sierra Divide, which is the watershed between east and west. Little precipitation happens here.

Reach a spot that descends to Deadman Pass at 2.4 miles and soon you come to the saddle. From here, the San Joaquin ridgeline gets slimmer, and you can gaze north by northwest to scout and plan your doable cross-country route to Two Teats. As you resume steady climbing, the views are more pronounced to the northwest, where Yosemite National Park's Mount Lyell, Donohue Peak, and Blacktop Peak march from south to north. There are many chances to peer down to the west into the origin of the San Joaquin River as the Middle Fork of the San Joaquin River flows smoothly into Agnew Meadow. A far-reaching panorama unfolds when you arrive at the tops of rounded Two Teats. Sprawling Mono Lake, an alkaline lake so laden with salt that you float in it without even moving, takes center stage to the northeast. They are topped in the far distance by the snowcapped White Mountains.

--2--

Burgers Animal Sanctuary

Total distance: Up to 6 miles
Hiking time: 3–5 hours
Difficulty: Moderate
Elevation gain: 1,300 feet
High point: 8,550 feet
Map: USGS Mount Dana
Information: Inyo National Forest

Mount Dana and Mount Gibbs, two of Yosemite National Park's most-noticed tall mountains, are prominently displayed throughout most of this route through a variety of eastern Sierra environments. View these picturesque peaks past quaking aspen groves, low sagebrush, large boulder outcrops, or lush vegetation along a scenic creek.

Mount Gibbs and Mount Dana from below Mono Dome

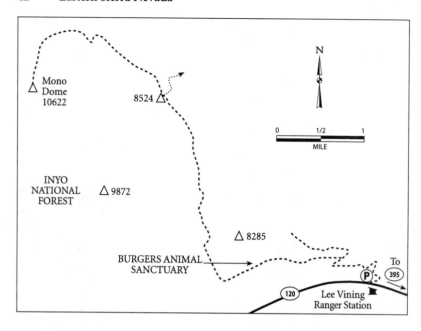

Although you may see a cross-country skier along the steady but gentle climb, chances are you'll enjoy the area all to yourself. The course follows the obvious road all the way, so routefinding is simple and staying with the route when it snows is doable. You may have to lug snowshoes a short distance if snow is scant.

Bighorn sheep have been relocated to this general vicinity, so look for their pointed, deerlike tracks in the snow. The uncommon pinyon pine is common on this route. Admire these shrubby, grayish green pines; they're the only ones around featuring single needles.

From Highway 395 just south of Lee Vining, travel west on Highway 120 (Tioga Road) for 1.2 miles to the right-hand turn on Log Cabin Road. If conditions permit, you can drive a short distance up to the snowline and park for free on the side of the road. Otherwise, park for free in the Forest Service ranger station lot across the highway.

It's a moderate grade up a sagebrush-covered and pinyon pine–dotted slope to begin. The views rotate between part of spacious Mono Lake to the east and rugged Mount Gibbs, Koip Crest, and 13,057-foot-tall Mount Dana to the southwest. At 0.8 mile from the highway, reach a road fork. Going right takes you some 3 miles to an awesome view of Mono Lake, but our course veers left and heads straight toward the picturesque east face of the Sierra Nevada and Mono Dome.

A series of signs tell you of the history of Burgers Animal Sanctuary, and the grade mellows as the trail follows along a willow-lined creek. The road bends sharply to the north around a rock cliff at 1.6 miles, and the views of Mounts Gibbs and Dana vanish. Promptly enter an extensive grove of quaking aspen called Robins Grove. Arrive at the cabins of the sanctuary 0.5-mile farther where signs tell you of the fauna and flora seen in this region.

Gradually enter moderate forest of fir, pine, and aspen as the snow-covered road parallels a lushly vegetated creek. Reach an old dam across the creek—as good a place as any to turn around. But from here, you can proceed up the road for another couple of bends, then pick and choose the safest cross-country route steeply up view-filled Mono Dome.

--ᢖ--

Lundy Lake to Oneida Lake

Total distance: 8 miles
Hiking time: 5–8 hours
Difficulty: Moderate
Elevation gain: 1,900 feet
High point: 9,655 feet
Maps: USGS Dunderberg Peak, USGS Lundy
Information: Toiyabe National Forest

When a sheet of white blankets Oneida Lake, and pockets of snow are gouged into the shapely mountains that encase this history-rich region, there is immense beauty and deep peace. Tucked into a confined cleft and capped with ominous peaks towering more than 1,500 feet above, three precious lakes will keep a curious snowshoer occupied for hours.

For history buffs, Crystal Lake features a lot of mining artifacts and structures remaining from the days of the May Lundy Mine. Routefinding on the old, snow-covered mining road is easy, even if you have to park at the end of the plowed road (extra hiking) rather than at the gate. Virtually every winter there's recent evidence of bent and broken trees, an indicator that avalanches have slid down the steep slopes, so call ahead to determine avalanche conditions.

East end of Lundy Lake

From Highway 395 some 18 miles south of Bridgeport at the junction with Highway 167, turn west on the road signed for Lundy Lake. Caltrans usually plows the first 1.5 miles of road, but if conditions permit, continue another 2.1 miles to the closed gate just before Lundy Lake and park for free near the restrooms.

Snowshoe up the road to Lundy Lake, where there are ideal photo opportunities a few yards west of the dam. From the gate, snowshoe the single-track mining road that climbs moderately above the south shores of Lundy Lake. Pass by an extensive colony of quaking aspens, then note that the route weaves in and out of desert chaparral such as mountain mahogany, sagebrush, tobacco brush, and currant. You'll pass through occasional moist seeps where deciduous shrubs, including elderberry, chokecherry, and willows, thrive. Over the first mile especially, there are constant views of snow-clad, metamorphic mountains that loom over long and lean Lundy Lake. Mount Olsen, at 11,086 feet, dominates to the northwest, and the tip of Black Mountain juts behind it. The sheer, mostly snow-free north face of Mount Scowden frowns at you from the west.

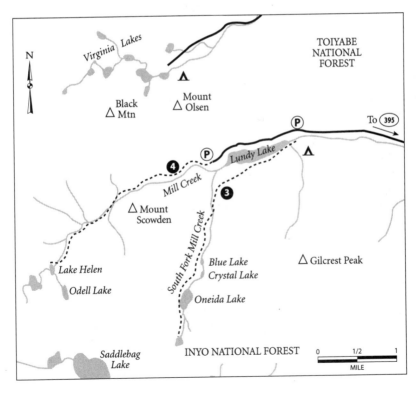

As the route abruptly veers south into Lake Canyon at 1.2 miles, you enter a forest of western white pine and red fir. The steady climb continues up this view-filled canyon, as you cross South Fork Mill Creek at 2.3 miles beneath lodgepole pines. The terrain now alternates between conifer forests and open areas. When the road levels, wander east to briefly check out tiny Blue Lake at 3.3 miles set in an open basin near the bottom of steep canyon walls.

A bit farther along the route, you reach a Y in the road. Take the left branch, which promptly leads to narrow Crystal Lake perched beneath sensational, steep cliffs. Scout the bevy of mining equipment and dilapidated structures scattered around the basin. Ore cars, rock walls, and huge tubs are among the extensive artifacts.

Back on the main snow-covered road, make a brief climb past a pile of tailings to the actual mine and take a set of tracks that still lead into an old, boarded-up shaft. Pick and choose your way from here to large and lovely Oneida Lake. Rolling terrain sprawling beyond the far shore climaxes with the stark and steep canyon walls of the Tioga Crest, forming a spectacular backdrop to the frozen expanse of rectangular Oneida Lake.

--4--

Lundy Canyon

Total distance: 6–10 miles
Hiking time: 5–7 hours
Difficulty: Moderate
Elevation gain: 1,100 feet
High point: 8,600 feet
Maps: USGS Lundy, USGS Dunderberg Peak
Information: Toiyabe National Forest

A soul can feel refreshingly lonely at the bottom of narrow and scenic Lundy Canyon in wintertime. The silence is occasionally interrupted, usually by another of a series of cascades and waterfalls that stream down its powerfully steep walls. Every step you take, a photo opportunity beckons over Lundy Lake or high up the plethora of 11,000-foot-plus peaks that punctuate the sky.

Routefinding on the old road and the snowshoe trail is easy, even if you have to park at the end of the plowed road (extra hiking) rather than at the gate. Whenever high-mountain canyons slice deeply into the vertical escarpment of tree-scant rocky slopes, avalanches can occur, and Lundy Canyon is no exception, so call ahead to determine avalanche conditions.

From Highway 395 some 18 miles south of Bridgeport at the junction with Highway 167, turn west on the road signed for Lundy Lake. Caltrans usually plows the first 1.5 miles of road, but if conditions permit, continue another 2.1 miles to the closed gate just before Lundy Lake and park for free (see map on page 45).

Snowshoe up the road to Lundy Lake, where great photos await a few yards west of the dam. Continue on the road on a level grade for a scenic 1.3 miles to the west end of Lundy Lake. Along the way, towering Mount Scowden's northeast face dominates from the southwest. Pass through Lundy Lake Resort, which is closed in the winter, climb briefly past the resort, draw near Mill Creek, come to some beaver ponds, then reach the Lundy Canyon trailhead proper.

Leave the snow-covered road and head up the canyon on a mild grade past a long array of white-trunked quaking aspens. Carefully ascend around a

Lundy Lake and Lundy Creek Canyon

steep wall that sports a waterfall, and soon cross a pair of side streams. Pass a final pond and continue in a light forest of red fir, lodgepole pine, and more aspen. You soon reach a large clearing 3 miles from the gate, where waterfalls tumble down the cliffs on both sides of the canyons.

As you continue to choose your own straightforward route along the bottom of the canyon, pause often to gaze northeast up at Mount Olsen, north for ominous Black Mountain, and northwest for 12,446-foot-tall Excelsior Mountain. When climbing intensifies, that's a signal that you're departing the canyon bottom and it's time to retrace your steps.

--5--

Virginia Lakes

Total distance: 8–14 miles
Hiking time: 6–9 hours
Difficulty: Moderate
Elevation gain: 1,500 feet
High point: 9,780 feet
Maps: USGS Dunderberg, USGS Lundy
Information: Toiyabe National Forest

Large colonies of quaking aspens, their bare limbs and white trunks becoming even brighter above a snow layer when the sun is out, surround the snowshoer on this tranquil and secluded route. On the way in to these subalpine lakes, the stark, barren, and snow-clad easternmost peaks and ridges greet you head on, punctuating the broad canyon bottom.

It's a steady but mostly gentle climb along snow-covered Virginia Lakes Road to a group of smallish lakes frozen solid. The pleasant scenery along most of the easy-to-follow course is wide-open, desert-motif terrain, where fragrant sagebrush dominates and is sometimes packed in white during periods of heavy snowfall. The dramatic backdrops of Black Mountain and Dunderberg Peak make for superb photos from the lakes.

Because of the exposed terrain and extra-high elevation, this trip should be avoided when foul weather and heavy winds kick up.

Travel to Conway Summit on Highway 395, which is 12 miles north of Lee Vining and 13 miles south of Bridgeport. Turn west on signed Virginia Lakes Road and follow it to the snow line, then park on the side of the road for free.

Mono County often plows the road almost all the way to the lakes in early spring, which allows cross-country skiers and snowshoers to venture farther up the Virginia Lakes canyon to explore gorgeous Cooney and Frog Lakes.

Follow the bending, gently to moderately climbing road, as it displays views sometimes to the northeast of Bridgeport Valley fronting the Sweetwater Mountains, occasionally south of Lee Vining Peak, and often to the west of Dunderberg Peak. Pass through typical eastside Sierra vegetation, mainly sagebrush and dead-looking (but alive) rabbit brush amid scattered lodgepole pines and sporadic clusters of aspens.

Draw near Virginia Creek at 1.5 miles and continue climbing a good ways above the north side of the stream. Pines and aspens fill in the scene more and more as Dunderberg Peak looms larger past the junction with Dunderberg

Willows, aspens, and Dunderberg Peak

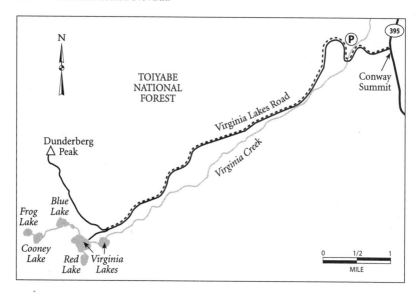

Meadow Road. A mild ascent ensues. Stay on Virginia Lakes Road past cabins to the largest of the Virginia Lakes at 5.7 miles. Open but rugged slopes rise up to 11,797-foot-tall Black Mountain to the southwest, making this lake scene dramatic. From here, Blue Lake is a mere 0.25 mile to the northwest, with Cooney and Frog Lakes beyond. Red Lake is located 0.3 mile to the south. Plan on spending a lot of time in this fabulously scenic area; perhaps you can build a snowman.

--*6*--

Robinson Creek to Barney Lake

Total distance: 8 miles
Hiking time: 5–7 hours
Difficulty: Moderate
Elevation gain: 1,200 feet
High point: 8,260 feet
Map: USGS Buckeye Ridge
Information: Toiyabe National Forest

Take a mellow, scenic, and secluded snowshoe stroll up orange- and rust-bottomed Robinson Creek past light forest and meadows to photogenic Barney

Robinson Creek and Barney Lake

Lake wedged in steep and ragged granite. Only the final 0.8 mile gains notable elevation and the terrain is easy to follow. Don't go if avalanche conditions are severe. Call ahead for the report.

From the town of Bridgeport on Highway 395, turn southwest onto signed Twin Lakes Road. Go 12.7 miles west on this paved road past both Twin Lakes to the entrance to Mono Village. Park for free along the side of the road.

Traipse through the camping area, following signs for Barney Lake. Reach an old fire road and promptly go right on the signed Barney Lake Trail in a quiet forest of Jeffrey pines, Sierra junipers, white firs, and aspens. The high-pitched purr of Robinson Creek accompanies you on a gentle climb past open areas sprinkled with snow-smashed sagebrush. Reach beaver ponds lined by aspens and a Hoover Wilderness sign at 2.7 miles, where there's a premium view to the south of rugged Little Slide Canyon.

It's an arduous climb away from Robinson Creek, eased by views behind you of Twin Lakes. Work your way up the slope near the creek. If the snow cover is heavy, you can proceed straight up the hillside over the brush. If snow is scant in spots, try to follow the snaking trail. The final ascent consists of a brief entry into cool pine forest before reaching 14-acre Barney Lake at 4.2 miles. With easy access to lake's edge for viewing 11,346-foot-tall Crown Point, Barney Lake at 8,290 feet in elevation makes for a prime picnic spot.

Barney Lake is encased in a deep-walled rocky basin, highlighted by dramatic Crown Point farther west up the canyon. Stark and steep granite slopes punctuated by scattered pines form a striking landscape. You have the option to explore farther up the canyon a mile or so, alternating between open, rocky sections and light forest dominated by graceful mountain hemlocks.

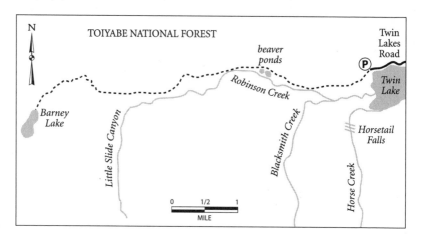

--7--

Twin Lakes

Total distance: Up to 9.5 miles
Hiking time: 4–6 hours
Difficulty: Easy
Elevation gain: 200 feet
High point: 7,200 feet
Map: USGS Twin Lakes
Information: Toiyabe National Forest

Filled with folks during summer, this matching pair of deep and gorgeous lakes transforms into a tranquil and remote wonderland when snow-covered in winter. This lightly forested shoreline route is pleasing to the eye the whole way, and it's ideal for novice snowshoers and cross-country skiers. Dramatic peaks rise suddenly above the lakes in all directions but east, some towering up to 4,000 vertical feet above the long and lean lakes.

The scattered trees and shrubbery and the open lakes offer ideal patrolling grounds for red-tailed hawks. Blue grouse hide in the bushes while Steller's jays squawk in the lower conifer limbs. Look for the gray-crowned rosy finch

Rabbitbrush, Twin Lake, and Crater Crest

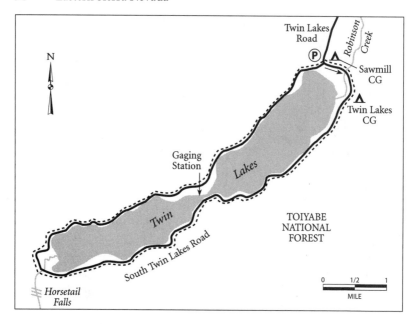

flittering in the pines or a wily coyote sneaking along the lake's edge. Try to spot animal tracks in the open areas, such as those of the long-tailed weasel.

Since the course is predictable and easy to follow, it can be negotiated while snow is falling or if the skies are low overcast. You can trudge along the southern shore for up to 4.5 miles and retrace your steps, especially if snow levels are low enough for vehicle traffic on the lake's north shore road. The trip can be reduced to a 4-mile loop in heavy snow by circumnavigating the lower lake.

From the town of Bridgeport on Highway 395, turn southwest onto signed Twin Lakes Road. After 9.5 miles on this paved road, reach the left-hand turn onto South Twin Lakes Road. Mono County periodically plows this road a short ways, so park for free on the side of the road or at the end of the plowed section as conditions allow.

Snowshoe along the extension of the roadway across the bridge over rust- and orange-bottomed Robinson Creek and proceed through Twin Lakes Campground. Stroll slowly along the east end of Lower Twin Lake and admire the serrated peaks forming Sawtooth Ridge to the southwest. Sagebrush is the dominant plant in open areas, while tall specimens of Jeffrey pines outnumber white firs and the occasional Sierra juniper.

This theme persists for the whole trip, as you wind clockwise around the south shore of Lower Twin Lake. The stark visage of Robinson Peak to the northwest opens up as you head westward, and 2 miles into the journey 11,732-foot-tall Victoria Peak farther west rules the landscape, backed with Hunewill Peak even farther west. If you loop around Lower Twin Lake or both lakes, Matterhorn Peak and Crater Crest to the east take center stage from the north shores.

Pickel Meadow

Total distance: Up to 5-mile loop
Hiking time: 3–4 hours
Difficulty: Easy
Elevation gain: 100 feet
High point: 6,760 feet
Map: USGS Pickel Meadow
Information: Toiyabe National Forest

Here's a classic example of an ordinary area transformed into an enchanted land when snow-covered. Families in snowshoes or on cross-country skis frolic along this simple route around the edges of expansive Pickel Meadow, with a few detours to its middle to admire the pure, rushing waters of meandering West Walker River.

No matter what time in winter you visit, something's bound to be peaking in rapture. It could be a heavier than normal snowpack tightly hemming the curving banks of the West Walker River. Or perhaps it might be the swollen, gleaming orange clusters of willows, standing naked in late winter with their new leaf buds about to burst. Or it could be a thin coating of snow, interspersed with frozen native bunchgrasses, dormant but heaving.

Because there's a substantial river flowing through the meadow, with colonies of willows in the middle and patches of forest on the edges, this route is ideal for spotting wildlife. If you're quiet and still, maybe a wily coyote will trot along an edge of a clearing. Porcupines sometimes cling to the main trunks of conifers, high up. The great horned owl resembles a big squatting cat, camouflaged in the evergreen boughs. Mountain chickadees flitter in the low limbs while Steller's jays squawk and rustle loudly in the branches. Deer herds come out late in the afternoon.

Novice snowshoers can let their guard down in the flat expanse of Pickel Meadow, while the more accomplished snowshoer can delve into the forest

Pickel Meadow

edges and explore the banks of the West Walker River a mere 0.25 mile away. Customizing wanderings to fit your fancy is easy here.

You may see soldiers from the nearby Mountain Warfare Training Center across the highway walking near the trailhead; otherwise, you're apt to have the whole meadow to yourself. Even weekends are a good time to go and still find privacy. Sonora Pass Highway is closed farther west, preventing the majority of traffic from passing through.

From north of Bridgeport on Highway 395, head west onto Sonora Pass Highway 108. Reach the Mountain Warfare Training Center after 3.6 miles, which is generally as far as Caltrans plows the highway in heavy snow seasons. But chances are you can drive another 1.3 miles to park for free near the locked gate that closes the highway. Just park alongside the highway as conditions allow.

Wander into Pickel Meadow and let your heart's desires dictate the route. If you can find a safe way to cross gorgeous West Walker River at the west end of the meadow, you can explore a mile or so up scenic Poore Creek before the terrain gets steeper. This can add another 2 miles to the trip.

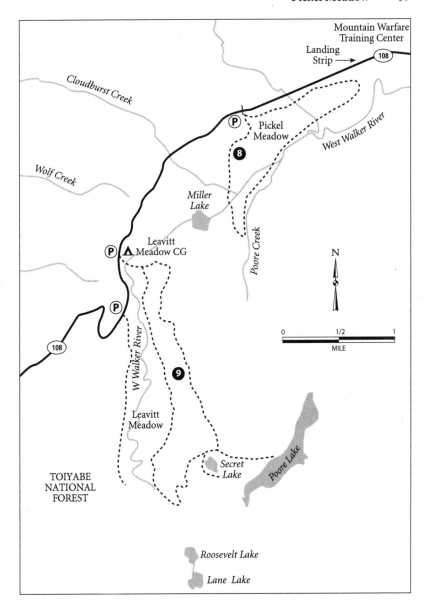

Rimmed by snow-clad ridges rising some 1,500 feet above the meadow, this area is rich in photo opportunities, especially when the sun sinks partially behind the mountains in late afternoon, casting dramatic shadows about the meadow.

-- 9 --

Leavitt Meadow: Poore Lake and Secret Lake

Total distance: 5–11 miles
Hiking time: 4–8 hours
Difficulty: Easy to moderate
Elevation gain: 700 feet
High point: 7,450 feet
Map: USGS Pickel Meadow
Information: Toiyabe National Forest

Deep peace and winter photo opportunities abound on this leisurely exploration of an exceptionally scenic high meadow and a shapely, large lake. Highlighted by the meandering course of crystal clear West Walker River and surrounded by snowy peaks and ridges, lovely Leavitt Meadow spans 2 miles and is 0.5-mile wide. Investigating the unspoiled shoreline of mile-long Poore Lake is doable and recommended, although it will add 1 mile or so to the already lengthy journey.

Once on this remote meadow, you can choose your own route and vary the length as energy and/or time dictates. By staying in Leavitt Meadow, you can bypass Secret Lake and Poore Lake and shave up to 3 miles from the trek, which is occasionally shared by cross-country skiers. Beginners will appreciate the flat terrain and all snowshoers will benefit from the obvious way, even when it's snowing. You may have to factor in an extra 2.2 miles to get there if the road is not passable, but following snow-covered Highway 108 is charming and tranquil.

From north of Bridgeport on Highway 395, head west onto Sonora Pass Highway 108 (see map on page 57). Reach the Mountain Warfare Training Center after 3.6 miles, and if snowpack is high, you'll have to give up your Leavitt Meadow plans, park here for free, and snowshoe the road 1.3 miles to explore Pickel Meadow (Route 8). But in many cases, you can continue to the pack station to park for free at Leavitt Meadow, 7.2 miles from Highway 395. Call ahead for snow conditions.

If you had to park at the gate 2.2 miles from the Leavitt Meadow trailhead, commence a gradual, winding climb along the snow-covered road, crossing quiet Wolf Creek after 0.3 mile. Check out the pleasing views across the canyon to the snow-covered slope above the West Walker River. At 1.4 miles, the road descends through a scattered pine forest down to the meadow.

Leavitt Meadow and West Walker River

Since West Walker River is usually difficult to cross, you may be confined to exploring its banks from the side you're already on, if you choose to explore just the meadow and not the lakes. Just head out on the meadow, past a cluster of corrals to the gently curving, willow-lined river. If the river is crossable, you can frolic in Leavitt Meadow and then negotiate the crossing of the river once you're on the south end of the meadow. The terrain requires some brief climbing sections over sagebrush and other dry vegetation that epitomizes the eastern Sierra as you pick and choose the easiest route east to the low basin that houses Poore Lake.

If taking the ridge above Leavitt Meadow to get to the lakes is your plan (thus avoiding crossing the river when it's too high), here's what to do: From the trailhead, follow the access road through the campground to the river bridge. Cross here, then wrap around some low hills on a moderate climb. Trudge past mountain mahogany, Jeffrey pine, and Sierra juniper to a trail sign with the West Walker River Trail 0.4 mile from the road. Bear left at the junction, reach a tiny meadow after a 200-yard climb, and then make a moderate ascent toward the crest of the ridge. For the next mile, there are delightful views of the Sweetwater Mountains and Pickel Meadow to the northeast, Leavitt Meadow below to the west, and Forsyth and Tower Peaks to the south. Just prior to the terrain dropping to Secret Lake 2.2 miles from the road, look for sprawling Poore Lake so you can plan the easiest access to it.

Descend through light forest 300 yards to the northeast shore of Secret Lake. This petite lake is surrounded by a rocky shoreline, and the steep and rocky cliffs on the other side of the lake form a photogenic backdrop. If you pick and choose your way down to Poore Lake (the last 0.25 mile is a bit steep), be sure to retrace your steps back to Secret Lake, where you traverse west to a junction. From here, you can head back up the ridge for a replay of those grand views, or skirt the eastern edge of Leavitt Meadow to the trailhead.

Half Dome and the Merced River

WESTERN SIERRA NEVADA

Yosemite Valley Area from Highway 41 to Highway 120

--*10*--

Badger Pass to Glacier Point

Total distance: 21 miles
Hiking time: 2–3 days
Difficulty: Strenuous
Elevation gain: 2,200 feet
High point: 7,830 feet
Maps: USGS Half Dome, USGS El Capitan
Information: Yosemite National Park

See the photogenic Yosemite Valley in a special way that only a few souls get to experience—from atop Glacier Point when it's hooded with snow. The thousands of tourists who drive to this popular vantage point in summer won't feel your cherished solitude and sense of major achievement, nor will they embrace the views that you'll encounter. Trek alongside the tracks of the groomed cross-country ski trail on Glacier Point Road during clear weather in winter or early spring and the peaceful and scenic memories will be forever etched in your spirit.

The anticipation of reaching the ambitious goal of Glacier Point will likely keep you energized and enthusiastic much of the way. After all, how often does anybody get to gaze 3,200 feet down into a valley bordered by stark granite and with a graceful river such as the Merced running through it? Along the way, you'll see plenty of picturesque, snow-capped sites, such as the nearby Clark Range, which rises above 11,000 feet in elevation.

From Wawona Road a few miles south of Yosemite Valley, turn east onto Glacier Point Road, drive 5 miles to Badger Pass Ski Area, and follow the blue signs to the upper parking lot, where you'll find the signed Glacier Point trailhead. Note that there is a $20 fee to get into Yosemite National Park, which buys you a pass that's good for 7 days.

Ascend the well-traveled, snow-covered road in a red fir forest for 1 mile to a sign for Dewey Point Ski Trail and stay straight. Continue a gentle climb for about 0.3 mile past Summit Meadow, then negotiate 1.5 miles worth of mildly twisting, slightly descending trail. Look for initial views of the Clark Range ahead, then stay straight at a signed junction at 2.8 miles. Make a brief ascent away from Peregoy Meadow, descend to cross Bridalveil Creek, and then climb moderately to another signed trail junction at 4 miles, where you stay left.

Continue east on the wide swath of the Glacier Point Road, climbing

White fir

moderately in a light Jeffrey pine forest interspersed with dead timber from the 1987 fire. Stay straight at another signed junction at 4.7 miles, and continue climbing as the route bends north, soon to reveal several clear views of the Clark Range, including Mount Clark, Gray Peak, Red Peak, and Merced Peak, stretching from north to south.

A steady ascent continues until the 7-mile point, where mostly flat terrain over the next 2 miles allows you to enjoy the plethora of views that unfold. Pass Pothole Meadow, then watch for hulking Sentinel Dome. The final mile consists of a twisting descent to Glacier Point, closely following the route of

Open forest along Glacier Point Road

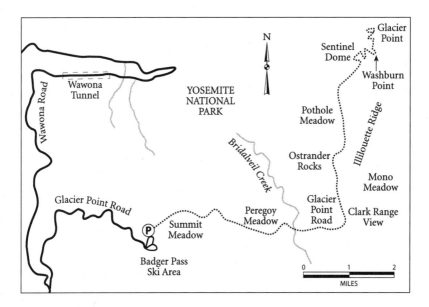

the original wagon road built in 1882. Gain the awesome vista at Washburn Point at 9.6 miles, featuring sweeping views of Mount Starr King and the Clark Range to the southeast and Half Dome to the northeast as well.

Get set for a whole new scene below when you reach the railing at Glacier Point. Sweeping east to west, gawk at Half Dome, North Dome, El Capitan, and Cathedral Rocks rising abruptly above U-shaped Yosemite Valley.

--11--

Ostrander Lake

Total distance: 20 miles
Hiking time: 11 hours or overnight
Difficulty: Moderate
Elevation gain: 2,000 feet
High point: 8,600 feet
Maps: USGS Half Dome, USGS Mariposa Grove
Information: Yosemite National Park

Dominated by snowy granite ridges and lined with conifers and granite slabs, 25-acre Ostrander Lake invites a stroll around its vase-shaped shoreline. Climb

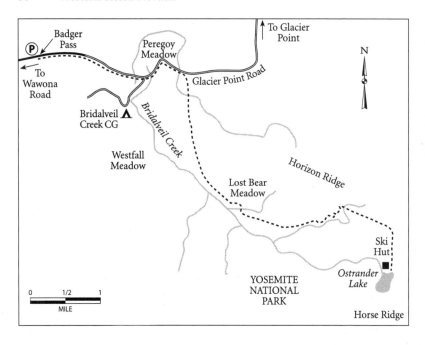

a mere 500 feet in elevation (check ahead for avalanche conditions) and mount Horse Ridge for inspirational views of snow-gouged Mount Starr King to the north and the entire Clark Range to the east.

This is a popular trip, especially during winter and spring weekends when large groups snowshoe or cross-country ski to the stone ski hut. Snowshoers and cross-country skiers can stay in Ostrander Hut if they've reserved it. For the most privacy, backpack in with snowshoes during the dead of winter on a weekday. With a mix of deep wild forest, numerous meadow strips, moving water, and a lake, this route offers a lot of chances to view wildlife. If you're planning on doing this all in one day, please be in good shape, leave at the crack of dawn, and be proactive about time factors.

To get there, drive to the signed Chinquapin junction from Wawona Road (also Highway 41). This junction is southwest of Yosemite Valley and northeast of Fresno. Turn northeast onto paved Glacier Point Road. Drive 5 miles to Badger Pass Ski Area, and follow the blue signs to the upper parking lot, where you'll find the signed Glacier Point trailhead. Note that a $20 fee is required to get into Yosemite National Park, which buys you a pass that's good for 7 days.

Ascend the well-traveled, snow-covered road in a red fir forest for 1 mile to the signed Dewey Point Ridge Trail and stay straight. Continue a gentle climb for 0.3 mile past Summit Meadow, then negotiate 1.5 miles worth of mildly twisting, slightly descending trail. Look for initial views of the Clark Range ahead, then stay straight at a signed junction at 2.8 miles. Make a brief ascent away from Peregoy Meadow, descend to cross Bridalveil Creek, and then climb moderately to another signed trail junction at 4 miles, where you leave Glacier Point Road and turn right for Ostrander Lake. Note that late in the snowshoe season Glacier Point Road may be cleared of snow, shortening your trip by 8 miles.

It's easy to get lost in a pleasant daydream over the first 3.5 miles from the turnoff, as the snow-covered route, a former jeep road, gently climbs through a forest interspersed with small meadows. These open areas are worth stopping at for a snack and/or drink and to sit quietly and wait for wildlife to come out. Coyotes occasionally sneak across these tiny meadows, and porcupines sometimes can be spotted high atop the conifers. Listen for the squawk of the Steller's jay and look for cute little dark-eyed juncos flittering quietly in the lower conifer boughs, sometimes shaking snow off the limbs when departing.

Two trail junctions on the right at 1.7 miles and 2.1 miles from the turnoff head promptly to Bridalveil Creek and its campground. To get up-close and personal with this peaceful stream that is very popular in the summer but generally people-free in snowshoe season, make a brief detour to it and then follow your tracks back to the route.

Steady and moderate ascent ensues in a forest rapidly recovering from a 1987 fire. The climb starts in a mixed conifer forest to an exposed slab that furnishes inaugural views of the sprawling, treed Bridalveil Creek basin. Enter a large and scattered stand of Jeffrey pine, then enter a forest of white firs, which are soon supplanted by red firs higher up, atop a saddle that bisects Horizon Ridge. Open stretches occur next, as your snow-covered, old jeep road snakes up the ridge amid sagebrush, which is often visible during light snow years or by late snowshoe season. You soon obtain extensive views spanning the Illilouette Creek drainage, where Mount Starr King rules. Half Dome, North Dome, Washington Column, and Royal Arches poke farther north, and their rocky tops are too steep to support much snow. The jagged pinnacles of the snow-capped Clark Range reign to the east.

Descend to the ski hut, which was built on a rocky, glacial moraine. Next to it, tucked in a bedrock basin sits typically dark gray Ostrander Lake. Camping is best along the west shore and fishing is relaxing, although it may be ice fishing in the deep of winter. Horse Ridge, an example of exfoliating granite, features an obvious overhanging temple to the south.

--*12*--

Tempo Dome and Westfall Meadows

Total distance: 6.4-mile loop
Hiking time: 4–8 hours
Difficulty: Moderate to strenuous
Elevation gain: 1,300 feet
High point: 7,845 feet
Map: USGS El Capitan
Information: Yosemite National Park

Capture countless views of pointed Clark Range, framed by regal red firs, and glide through a large and peaceful meadow on this mostly quiet and remote snowshoe venture. Because there are other more popular routes in the Badger Pass area, and since this route starts out with a hefty climb followed by a lot of little ups and downs, you're apt to have this trekking treat to yourself. Cross-country skiers occasionally share the route.

Clark Range from Tempo Dome

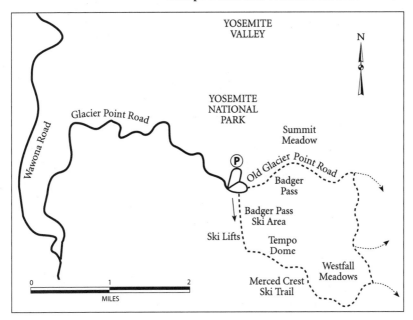

From Wawona Road a few miles south of Yosemite Valley, turn east onto Glacier Point Road, drive 5 miles to Badger Pass Ski Area, and follow the blue signs to the upper parking lot, where you'll find the signed Glacier Point trailhead. The trailhead begins at the "Eagle" chairlift.

Creep slowly upward alongside the chairlift, smiling politely whenever someone in a moving chair above you ridicules your hard work. After 0.8 mile and 600 vertical feet of climbing, reach the ridge top and promptly find the signed Merced Crest Ski Trail. Progress along the open crest for 0.2 mile, followed by a brief descent and then a short climb to reach Tempo Dome at 1.3 miles. From intermittent clearings in the forest, check out impressive vistas of the Clark Range to the east and the granitic mountains above Little Yosemite Valley to the southeast, including the less-steep visage of Half Dome.

Continue to check out the views as you drop off the back side of Tempo Dome and back into a light red fir and Jeffrey pine forest. The denser the forest sections, the more you have to watch for the rectangular yellow markers to stay on your route. After a trio of ups and downs, views vanish for a while as you descend diagonally across the mountainside. Continue down toward the basin south of Westfall Meadows, getting to a signed trail junction at 2.5 miles. Your course curves north and promptly enters a small pocket meadow. After a brief stint in light forest, you set foot in graceful Westfall Meadows at 2.8 miles.

Get lost in a daydream as you stroll effortlessly across the expansive, scenic, and isolated meadow. Follow the left-hand branch of clearing into the trees at the end of the meadow at 3.7 miles and climb mildly through forest to the gap. Descend to the north for 0.3 mile into a narrow meadow, then turn left on the snow-covered Old Glacier Point Road. Follow all signs west to Badger Pass over the final 2.1 miles.

--13--

Mirror Lake and Tenaya Creek

Total distance: Up to 6 miles loop
Hiking time: 4–6 hours
Difficulty: Easy
Elevation gain: 200 feet
High point: 4,100
Map: USGS Half Dome
Information: Yosemite National Park

If you can make only one snowshoe trip in Yosemite, let this be the one. Astonishing views of stark granite peaks and domes, scenic creekside strolling, and an aptly named lake that reflects its mountainous surroundings, this route offers a lot at little energy expense.

Rust colored, boulder-strewn Tenaya Creek is a precious gem of a stream that gets lovelier and more remote with each step east of Mirror Lake. Everyone assumes that since popular Half Dome looms triumphantly above Mirror Lake that its vertical face reflected in Mirror Lake takes center stage, but it's Mount Watkins to the east that is often photographed in the lake's shallow and usually calm waters.

Actually, Mirror Lake is well on its way to becoming a meadow, and winter and early spring are the best times to capture the essence of the lake and its famous reflected images before it dries up. Hundreds of years ago, huge boulders tumbled down the steep mountain and partially dammed Tenaya Creek, helping to form this large pool.

You may have to carry snowshoes some of the way to the often populated lake, but Tenaya Canyon above the lake usually has a deeper snowpack that lingers longer. Call ahead for snow conditions. The mostly level grade, along with the notion that you can't get lost as long as you stay in the canyon bottom, makes this a suitable trek for snowshoers and cross-country skiers ready to break away from easier, marked trails.

Basket Dome from Mirror Lake

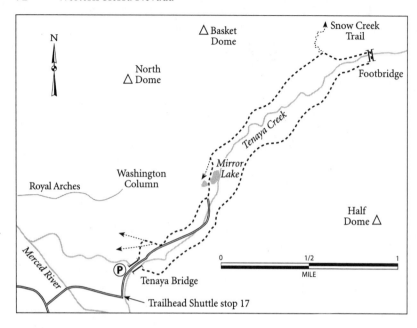

Make your way to Yosemite National Park east from I-5 by taking Highway 120 just south of Stockton, Highway 140 in Merced, or Highway 41 in Fresno. Once in the park (a $20 fee is charged for a 7-day pass), follow all signs into Yosemite Valley. Drive to Lower Pines Campground or Curry Village and park in one of the lots. The trailhead is the paved road that heads east.

It's a pleasant 1.2-mile-long stroll in an open forest bordering meandering Tenaya Creek to willow- and alder-lined Mirror Lake. As you explore the shapely shoreline, gaze up to the rocky crevices in the cliffs looming over the lake to the south, knowing there are several prime nesting nooks for spotted bats and peregrine falcons, two of Yosemite Park's endangered species. Swifts, swallows, and ouzels also inhabit the steep, granitic flanks.

Getting around the lake and surrounding meadow covers 0.4 mile. Listen for the chorus of croaking Pacific tree frogs in the mushy meadow just above the lake's eastern shore. As you ascend gently up the canyon, look for patches of bracken fern, once used by the local Indians to make baskets.

Beyond the meadow, your route passes through a rock slide below stark granite cliffs, where the nicest views are behind to the left and across the canyon of Half Dome. Reenter light forest of ponderosa pine, incense cedar, and Douglas fir and follow Tenaya Creek for a short while. Reach a junction at 2.8 miles, where you either turn around or bear right to make a loop trip, soon crossing a footbridge over Tenaya Creek.

--*14*--

Yosemite Valley: Yosemite Falls and Royal Arches

Total distance: 6.5-mile loop
Hiking time: 4–7 hours
Difficulty: Easy to moderate
Elevation gain: 600 feet
High point: 4,175 feet
Maps: USGS Half Dome, USGS Yosemite Falls
Information: Yosemite National Park

Gaze upon the farthest-falling falls in America, stand beneath a vertical wall of sheer granite that towers nearly 2,000 feet above you, stroll through a scenic meadow, and visit a wild river on this unforgettable trek.

Snowshoeing this route on a weekday is probably the easiest way to explore the numerous photogenic sites rock-walled Yosemite Valley offers, minus the major crowds of tourists. This is a unique trip, for you can snowshoe to or near Yosemite Falls, Royal Arches, Ahwahnee Meadow, and the meandering Merced River, and have lunch at a restaurant roughly halfway through.

Half Dome and Merced River

Yosemite Falls seen from Merced River

Your course adjoins the easternmost main valley roads, where interpretive signs posted near turnouts tell you of the interesting geology of the area. An occasional cross-country skier may glide by and your route alternates between busy, developed areas and sections of rapturous solitude. Call ahead for road and snow conditions.

Drive to Yosemite National Park east from I-5 by taking Highway 120 just south of Stockton, Highway 140 in Merced, or Highway 41 in Fresno. Once in the park (a $20 fee is charged for a 7-day pass), follow all signs into Yosemite Valley.

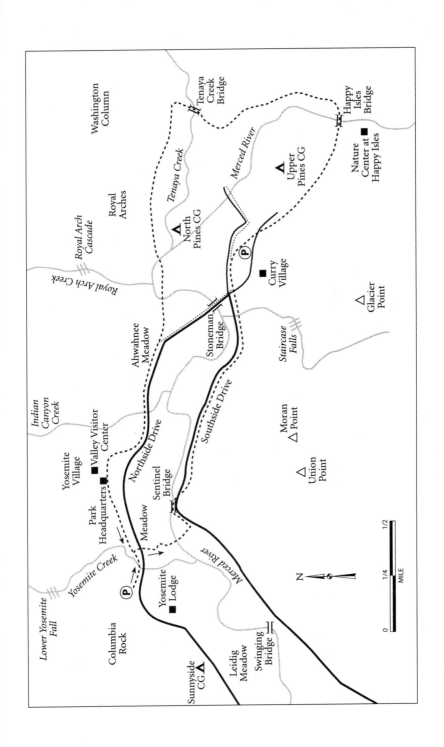

Make your way to Yosemite Falls Parking Lot (your starting point) by taking the shuttle bus from Curry Village (runs every 20 minutes) or by driving if there's ample clearing.

To start, head east toward Yosemite Village on the pedestrian path. At 0.2 mile, turn south, crossing Northside Drive while heading out into a meadow. As you cross shallow, orange-bottomed Merced River via a footbridge, admire views of the river and Half Dome to the east. Behind the chapel at 0.5 mile, find the trail junction and turn east. Wander through an area of black oaks and big boulders, and soon enter an evergreen forest of incense cedar, Douglas fir, and ponderosa pine, a theme that disappears and reappears throughout the journey as you more or less pick and choose your route around the outer edges of Yosemite Valley.

Reach the outskirts of Curry Village at 2.5 miles, pass the hamburger stand and then Upper Pines Campground to your left. Cross the Happy Isles Bridge spanning the Merced River, pass underneath a huge overhanging rock, and eventually reach a trail junction near the Tenaya Bridge, where you turn left, crossing the closed road to Mirror Lake at 3.4 miles.

Fine views of steep and granitic Royal Arches are yours as you walk along Tenaya Creek, soon reaching the stables at 3.8 miles, where you bear sharply right near the sign for Yosemite Falls. As you angle west in light forest, note improved views of Royal Arches punctuating the sky as you drop down to skirt scenic Ahwahnee Meadow at 4.6 miles. Over the next 2 miles, consisting of a moderate descent, ascent, and then mostly level trekking, watch for views to the north of Yosemite Falls, which free-fall 2,425 feet.

--*25*--

Yosemite Valley: El Capitan and Bridalveil Falls

Total distance: 11-mile loop
Hiking time: 6–11 hours
Difficulty: Easy to moderate
Elevation gain: 500 feet
High point: 4,065 feet
Maps: USGS Half Dome, USGS Yosemite Falls
Information: Yosemite National Park

When snow occasionally blankets the Yosemite Valley and wedges in the stark and vertical granite walls, a special and unforgettable encounter awaits. The

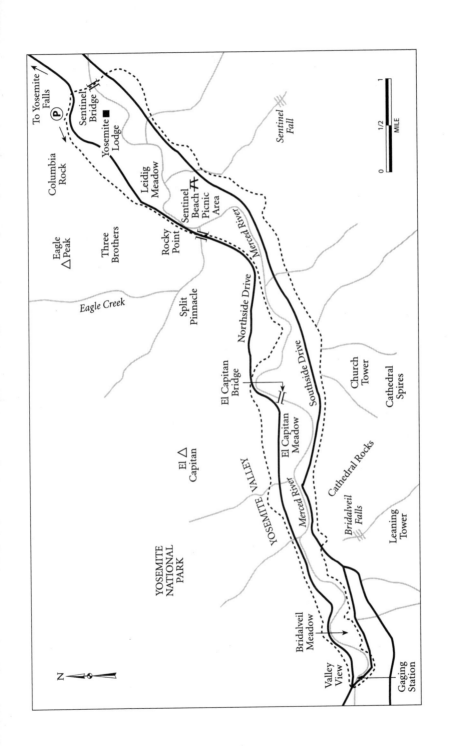

keys are good timing (there's enough snow perhaps 20 to 40 days a year) and staying more than a day, for there are so many breathtaking sites to explore.

This route displays the photogenic splendor of a gargantuan granite chunk of mountain called El Capitan, towering above shallow and scenic Merced River. Mix in views like Bridalveil Falls, free-falling from the shoulder of massive Cathedral Rocks, and the journey becomes an epic wonderland of continuous and awesome picturesque highlights.

Your course adjoins the main valley roads, where interpretive signs posted near turnouts tell you of the interesting geology of the area. An occasional cross-country skier may glide by. To avoid the crowds, come in midweek. Call ahead for road and snow conditions.

Drive to Yosemite National Park east from I-5 by taking Highway 120 just south of Stockton, Highway 140 in Merced, or Highway 41 in Fresno. Once in the park (a $20 fee is charged for a 7-day pass), follow all signs into Yosemite Valley. Make your way to Yosemite Falls Parking Lot (your starting point) by taking the shuttle bus from Curry Village (runs every 20 minutes) or by driving there if there's ample clearing.

Find the Valley Loop Trail behind the restroom and head south by southwest on mostly level grade, which stays that way to journey's end. Traipse in a light forest of incense cedar, ponderosa pine, Douglas fir, and black oak, an intermittent theme on this trek. Pass above Sunnyside Campground, and then head for and cross the main road. Admire Leidig Meadow at 1.2 miles as you skirt past it, then approach icy clear Merced River, which is mostly rock-bottomed and features a brownish orange cast. Find a good perch for looking east at a scene that includes North Dome, Royal Arches, Clouds Rest, and Half Dome.

Cross Eagle Creek via a wooden bridge and head for the small clearing that reveals a staggering view of precipitous El Capitan. This massive bulk of durable, unbroken granite soars 3,000 feet into the sky. The Ahwahnechee Indian name for El Capitan is Tutokanula for an inchworm that, according to legend, led bear cubs safely down the sheer cliff. Varying and arguably better views of El Capitan keep coming as you follow the peaceful course of alder- and willow-lined Merced River. Pass the El Capitan Picnic Area at 3.3 miles, snowshoe beneath the looming mountain itself a mile farther, and then cross Ribbon Creek.

Plan on picnicking at a photogenic spot called Valley View at 5.4 miles. By wandering along the banks of a rapids section of Merced River, you can capture smallish Bridalveil Meadow topped in the same gaze by El Capitan, Clouds

El Capitan from Merced River

Rest, and Half Dome. Switch your stare to the south and spy slim but powerful Bridalveil Falls pouring and misting straight down a stark granite face. The Ahwahnechee called this place Pohono, "Spirit of the Puffing Wind." The wind swirls about the cliff, occasionally lifting the spray as it eventually plummets several hundred feet.

Stand on the Pohono Bridge at roughly the halfway point, cross it, and continue to pick and choose your way counterclockwise. Close-up views of Bridalveil Falls occur at 6.7 miles as you crane your neck upward to the imposing Cathedral Rocks, a darker gray than most of the massive granite rocks found here. View El Capitan beyond close-by Merced River and El Capitan Meadow 1 mile farther. Just before reaching Sentinel Bridge at 10.7 miles, which you cross to get back to the trailhead, your attention will be fixed on Yosemite Falls to the northeast. It's the longest-falling falls in America—fifth longest in the world at 2,425 feet.

--*16*--
Inspiration Point and Stanford Point

Total distance: 2.5 miles for Inspiration Point; 8 miles for Stanford Point
Hiking time: 3–9 hours
Difficulty: Strenuous
Elevation gain: From 1,000 to 3,300 feet
High point: 6,950 feet
Map: USGS El Capitan
Information: Yosemite National Park

Some folks must have a special place to themselves, even if it means a lot of climbing and forging their own path. If this sounds like you, sign up here for a challenging but doable snowshoe route up a north-facing flank of Yosemite Valley that leads to jaw-dropping views of major place names normally seen by throngs of tourists below.

For those who are a bit less than totally fit, make your goal Inspiration Point, the original view of the valley for travelers along the old Wawona wagon road. For energetic and toned souls who want even more seclusion and better views, press on to Stanford Point. The hope is that someone before you accomplished the routefinding task and laid out snowshoe tracks to follow. Otherwise, you must negotiate the signed Pohono Trail as best as possible in a light to medium forest via switchbacks at first, then more or less straight up the

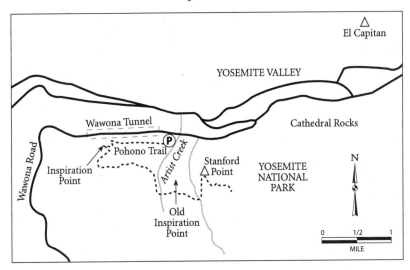

mountainside farther on. The key is to go on a mostly sunny day so you can see far enough ahead to always choose the easiest and safest route, especially if you've temporarily lost Pohono Trail—a summer path. The way basically heads up the least steep part of the slope, first westerly for about 1.5 miles, then southeast for a couple miles. If there's not enough snow at the start, you may have to lug your snowshoes for a distance. Call ahead for snow conditions.

You'll need to first get to Yosemite National Park, which is east from I-5, by taking Highway 120 just south of Stockton, Highway 140 in Merced, or Highway 41 in Fresno. Once in the park (a $20 fee is charged for a 7-day pass), follow all signs into Yosemite Valley and then Wawona Road. Drive to the east end of Wawona Tunnel on Wawona Road, and park in the south lot across from Discovery View.

At first, climb steadily past shrubby canyon live oak, incense cedar, ponderosa pine, Douglas fir, black oak, and large specimens of whiteleaf manzanita. Sporadic gaps in the forest cover allow teasing glimpses of Bridalveil Falls, El Capitan, and Half Dome punctuating Yosemite Valley. Cross an abandoned road at 0.6 mile. Built in 1875, this was the original wagon route to Yosemite Valley. Continue switchbacking through forest as the live oak, black oak, and manzanita begin to disappear.

Reach a pair of metal signs at 1.3 miles that indicate Inspiration Point. Cedars and pines interrupt your view here, but a brief scamper west followed by a short descent to the edge of some cliffs renders a spectacular view. Stretching north to south, check out El Capitan, snow-clad Clouds Rest, Half

Ponderosa pines and El Capitan

Dome, Sentinel Dome, and Cathedral Rocks. The enormous weight and erosive power of moving ice spiked with rock fragments plowed wide the former V-shaped Yosemite Valley and carved these stark granite walls.

Light forest soon takes over as the route bends and zigzags up the mountainside. Cross a small creek, continue ascending across the mountain face, and climb more steeply just before reaching Artist Creek at 2.6 miles. You can scramble northeast 0.25 mile to Old Inspiration Point, gather your fantastic views, and call it a day if you like. Our route veers eastward, and soon you're rewarded with opening views as you climb out of forest into more open country. Skirt around a rock promontory at 3.5 miles, then gradually descend northward toward tempting Stanford Point, which you reach 0.5 mile farther. All the previously mentioned views simply become more commanding, pronounced, and jaw-dropping here.

--*17*--
Tuolumne Grove and Hodgdon Meadow

Total distance: 6 miles one way; 2.8 miles round trip for Tuolumne Grove
Hiking time: 2–4 hours
Difficulty: Easy to moderate
Elevation gain: 500 feet
High point: 6,200 feet
Map: USGS Ackerson Mountain
Information: Yosemite National Park

Here's an ideal opportunity to stand alone beneath the world's largest living things while breathing clear and cool, snowy season air. Time your visit just after fresh snowfall and these mighty giant sequoia trees wear mystical white beards.

Tuolumne Grove is the most popular of the three giant sequoia groves gracing Yosemite National Park. But by extending the journey 4 more miles downhill to Hodgdon Meadow and the Big Oak Flat Entrance Station, you benefit from the most overall seclusion of the three hikes. To hike the one-way version of this route, you'll need to hitch a ride back to the trailhead or prearrange a car shuttle pick-up.

Join cross-country skiers on this all-downhill endeavor to admire these hulking trees, among the rarest in America. Discover the bizarre-looking Dead Giant (tunneled in 1878).

Sequoias

Drive to the junction of Crane Flat with the Tioga Road. It's 9 miles northwest of the junction with Highway 140 and 7.3 miles southeast of the Big Oak Flat Entrance Station. Follow the Tioga Road (Highway 120) 0.6 mile to the large parking area near the sign for Tuolumne Grove. A $20 fee is charged to get into Yosemite National Park, which buys a pass that's good for 7 days.

Downhill snowshoeing in a pleasant mixed forest ensues right from the start. Note the varying sizes of young and old white firs. Gradually, incense cedars and sugar pines join the conifer forest and remain for the rest of the way. After numerous sharp bends along Old Big Oak Flat Road, you sweep around a hillside and enter Tuolumne Grove at 1.1 miles.

A short lateral spur trail to the right leads promptly to the Tunnel Tree, which reveals the cinnamon-colored trunks typical of sequoias. This quaint tree has a huge, teepee-shaped hole in its base and a top resembling a tuning fork. With your head tilted way back, wander through this cluster of about 25 sequoias, looking down occasionally to read the interpretive signs.

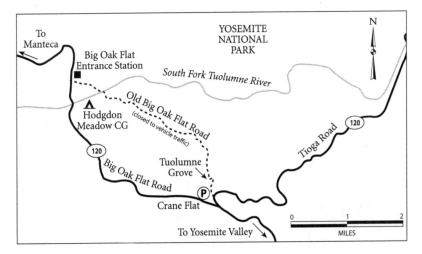

Once the visions of the sequoias' extreme girth is totally etched into your memory, either climb the road back to your car or continue downhill along Old Big Oak Flat Road (briefly described next). As you appreciate groves of rather sizable white firs, replay the enticing sequoia scene in your mind. Before you know it, you've spent about 90 minutes of tranquil snowshoeing, perhaps being watched by a great horned owl perched in the evergreen boughs above. Then you arrive at small but scenic Hodgdon Meadow at 5.5 miles, where it's another 0.5 mile to Big Oak Flat Entrance Station and the visitor center.

--*18*--

Crane Flat Lookout

Total distance: 3.2 miles
Hiking time: 2–3 hours
Difficulty: Easy
Elevation gain: 500 feet
High point: 6,645 feet
Map: USGS Ackerson Mountain
Information: Yosemite National Park

An easy yet remote climb leads to Crane Flat Lookout, where an enticing panorama of Yosemite National Park's upper reaches and other Sierra Nevada await. Still manned during times of high fire danger, impressively built Crane

Clark Range from Crane Flat Lookout

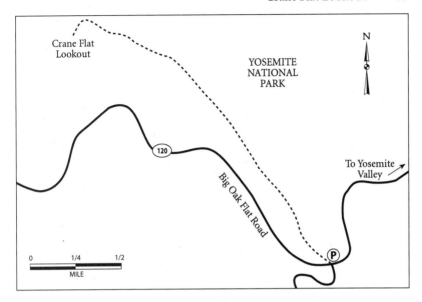

Flat Lookout sits on a large plain that beckons a snowshoer to venture to every corner to see what view's in store. The route's popular with cross-country skiers as well.

Get to the trailhead by driving Big Oak Flat Road (Highway 120) 6.8 miles southeast from the Big Oak Flat Entrance or 9.3 miles northwest of the junction with Highway 140. A $20 fee is charged for entrance into Yosemite National Park, which buys you a pass that's good for 7 days. Therefore, when you come here, it's a good idea to stick around at least a couple of days to snowshoe the many routes the park features (see adjoining entries).

To start, it's a steady 0.25-mile climb followed by a brief descent in a mixed forest of sugar pine, ponderosa pine, white fir, incense cedar, and Douglas fir. The sizes are an equal mix of short, medium, and tall, casting intricate and dappled shade patterns on the snow. Peaceful and steady ascent ensues in this lovely forest, where mule deer and coyote tracks occasionally are spotted on the old, snow-covered road.

A brief but intense climb occurs at 1.3 miles, near the summit. The terrain switches to open countryside with drifts of manzanita near and at the top.

As you wander the edges of Crane Flat Lookout's flat zenith scanning the vast scenery, note that the best views are far off (consider bringing binoculars). The most impressive view is the tall Clark Range and Half Dome to the southeast. Peruse the conifer-clad range that hides the Merced River Canyon to the south.

--*19*--

Merced Grove

Total distance: 3 miles
Hiking time: 2–3 hours
Difficulty: Easy
Elevation gain: 500 feet
High point: 5,840 feet
Map: USGS Ackerson Mountain
Information: Yosemite National Park

Experience deep peace and associate with the world's largest things with a snow-shoe trip down into Yosemite National Park's smallest of three sequoia groves. Among the rarest trees in America, these giant sequoias will most likely give you the same emotions and feelings as being among their close relatives, the mammoth redwoods of the Northern California coast.

Check ahead to ensure there's enough snow at this elevation and join cross-country skiers on a quiet and isolated snowshoe trip to a few clusters of stately sequoias called Merced Grove. Afterward, consider snowshoeing to nearby Tuolumne Grove (Route 17) to admire about 25 more sequoias and to extend your snowshoe endeavor to about 6 miles round trip. By far the most remote of the three groves, Merced Grove is a prime resource study area for learning more about sequoias.

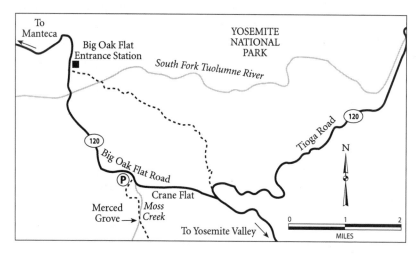

Jeffrey pine

The parking lot for Merced Grove trailhead is on the southwest side of Highway 120, about 4 miles south of the Big Oak Flat Entrance and 3.5 miles west of the junction at Crane Flat.

The easy-to-discern route follows a closed road all the way down to the grove in a scenic forest of incense cedar, ponderosa pine, and white fir. Look for long-tailed weasel, mule deer, and raccoon tracks in the snow. Bear left at a Y junction at 0.6 mile, then note how the descent becomes more obvious. The old road winds around and emerges into the drainage of Moss Creek. The route heads down to the tumbling creek, then reaches the first cluster of sequoias where the grade lessens. They're in a row of six, with a handful more scattered behind on the hillside.

It's possible for some of these trees to live up to 3,000 years, perhaps eventually reaching heights of 250 feet and a trunk girth of 30 feet. Growing exceptionally fast throughout their lives, these big trees are resistant to death from fire, and some of these sequoias here have already survived lightning strikes. Fire suppression and logging from the past are the biggest contributors to the decline in sequoias.

The route curves and reaches more sequoias 100 yards farther at 1.5 miles.

Red Lake Peak

NORTHERN SIERRA NEVADA

Carson Pass Area near Highway 88

--20--

Silver Lake

Total distance: Up to 5 miles
Hiking time: 2–4 hours
Difficulty: Easy
Elevation gain: 200 feet
High point: 7,400 feet
Map: USGS Caples Lake
Information: Amador Ranger District, Eldorado National Forest

Teardrop-shaped Silver Lake is one of the surprise snowshoe secrets in the Mokelumne Wilderness Area. Intimately tracing the curving shoreline, this route offers unexpected privacy and a lot of chances to see wildlife such as Steller's jays, red-tailed hawks, and great horned owls. Bustling with tourists in the warm season, the trek around all or part of snow-clad Silver Lake in the privacy of midwinter is a delightful alternative to Carson Pass, which most snowshoers explore instead.

Loaded with views of Martin Point, Thunder Mountain, and other Sierra Nevada peaks, the counterclockwise journey around Silver Lake is occasionally shared by cross-country skiers or even hikers who've hopefully waterproofed

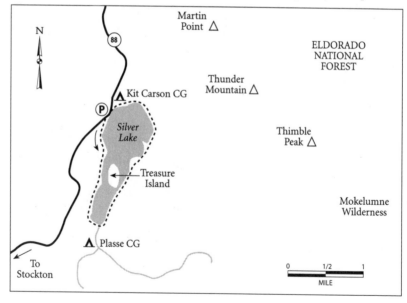

View of Thunder Mountain and Martin Point from Silver Lake

their boots. The easy, pick-and-choose route is forgiving on days of inclement weather. Unless there are major snow accumulations, be safe and avoid venturing out on the lake. When the snow level is low, granite slabs, big boulders, and miniature rocky beaches are exposed, adding a nice twist to your outing. Silver Lake is also known for its exciting ice fishing.

To get there, take Highway 88 to 5 miles west of Kirkwood, then turn south on Kays Road. Drive 0.3 mile and park for free next to Silver Lake Resort alongside the orange markers.

Mosey south along the western shore amid lodgepole pines and twisted, leaning Sierra juniper trees. With rough and chunky trunks, some of the junipers power their way through cracks and spaces between huge boulders and slabs. This odd mix of conifers in an open forest setting accompanies you the whole way. Within 0.25 mile, sights and most of the sounds of Highway 88 are gone.

After 0.5 mile, look for a photogenic clearing framed by conifers for peering at the brownish, steep flanks of Martin Point and Thunder Mountain to the northeast, across the widest segment of Silver Lake. At 1.2 miles, rectangular

Treasure Island is a bit more than a stone's throw away, decorating the lake directly east.

Weave in and out of forests and flat clearings and soon reach both inlet creeks from the far southern shore at 2.3 miles. Most folks are naturally enticed to cross, see new country, and complete the loop past two campgrounds for a full 5 miler. If the creeks are too high, double back, but take a varying course from before so that you'll see more visual highlights. The views are actually better from the western shore anyway, so you're not missing a whole lot. Be sure to visit at least a couple of the driftwood-lined, pebbly pocket beaches.

--21--

Caples Lake and Emigrant Lake

Total distance: 9 miles
Hiking time: 5–8 hours
Difficulty: Moderate
Elevation gain: 1,100 feet
High point: 8,600 feet
Map: USGS Caples Lake
Information: Amador Ranger District, Eldorado National Forest

Rarely do two lakes on one snowshoe journey vary so much. Hat-shaped Caples Lake, which you stroll the shores of for more than 2 miles, is huge, often populated with cross-country skiers, and often partly to mostly melted during snowshoe season. Slug-shaped Emigrant Lake, your ultimate destination, is about 0.3 mile long, partially encased by granite walls, extremely remote, and heavily covered in snow even late in the season.

It's a lengthy and leisurely shaded ramble along the southern shore of shapely Caples Lake, then trace willow-lined Emigrant Creek past snowy meadows to glacier-formed Emigrant Lake. Tall Mokelumne Wilderness peaks tower above this deep and secluded lake. Fishermen sometimes try ice fishing in both lakes.

Drive to Caples Lake Dam (some 100 miles east of Stockton) on the south side of Highway 88, and park for free. If this lot is jammed (which can happen on sunny weekends) or snow-packed, you may have to choose a spot safely off the side of Highway 88 to park, then carefully carry your snowshoes to the spillway. Another option is to head west of the dam for 0.4 mile and park at the Kirkwood Cross Country Ski Center. In this case, it's always best to ask permission.

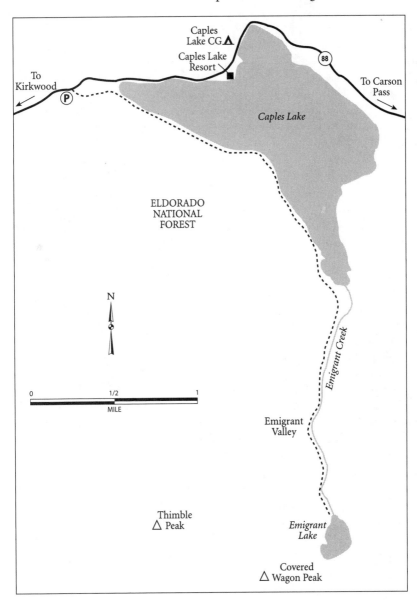

Your mission is to stay intimately close to the shore of Caples Lake to just before its southeastern corner. Elephants Back (a bald and smooth mountain) looms to the east way beyond some quaking aspen trees at the hike's onset. Stroll in and out of shade supplied by lodgepole pines near water's edge and

Round Top and Caples Lake

red firs just offshore. The ridgeline to the north features Little Round Top (see Snowshoe Route 22) and stays in view for a couple miles, past an understory of currants.

Mighty Round Top, the area's highest peak, shows its ominous head as you reach a long clearing at 1.3 miles. Pass through a small grove of quaking aspen, then cross four seasonal creeks over the next 1.2 miles. Veer away from Caples Lake and angle south along frigid Emigrant Creek.

Climb gently through small meadow patches and past granite outcrops and boulders. Mountain hemlock soon joins the forest near the creek bank at 3.4 miles. Continue to head up the drainage of Emigrant Creek, staying to the left of a rock promontory. The climb intensifies for 0.5 mile, eased by views to the east of The Sisters' rocky spires. The route levels at 4.3 miles and parallels a small meadow near the stream.

After another 0.25 mile, reach granite-ringed Emigrant Lake. A steep and rugged talus-clad cliff rises from the lake's south shore, and 9,565-foot-high Covered Wagon Peak stands guard to the southwest. At 9,805 feet, Thimble Peak towers farther west. This volcanic vent covered much of the surrounding area with lava, mudflows, and volcanic ash from 4 to 20 million years ago. Lodgepole pine and mountain hemlock furnish splashes of shade as you explore the shoreline of Emigrant Lake. Avalanche debris usually piles up at the base of the cirque cliffs at the head of the canyon.

--22--

Little Round Top

Total distance: 10 miles
Hiking time: 5–7 hours
Difficulty: Moderate
Elevation gain: 1,200 feet
High point: 9,590 feet
Maps: USGS Caples Lake, USGS Carson Pass
Information: Amador Ranger District, Eldorado National Forest

It's a wide open ridge route to Little Round Top, a series of staggered bumps to climb atop or skirt around. This "call-your-own-shots" journey lets you bag any bumpy peak you pick along the way, and you can turn back once you've savored enough far-reaching vistas showing off the Carson Pass area. Of course,

Little Round Top

these forever-changing views are so seductive, you're apt to be sitting atop Little Round Top with a satisfied smile before you know it.

This secret course to wild and spacious high country is known to a few cross-country skiers and patrolled by the red-tailed hawk and the wily coyote. Look down on several lakes, with sky blue Lake Tahoe glimmering to the north. The other lakes are apt to be snow-covered, resembling white meadows in disguise.

From Carson Pass on Highway 88, drive 0.2 mile west and park on the north side of the highway in Meiss Meadow Sno-Park. To obtain your pass, call (209) 258-7248.

Begin by heading west past a couple of hiking signs, generally contouring the lightly forested slopes. Grotesquely shaped, large specimens of Sierra juniper look even more peculiar interspersed with random colonies of quaking aspens that mingle with red fir and lodgepole pines. Bend your way into a modest drainage, then head for the obvious saddle to the north. The bare terrain offers awesome views to the south of Elephants Back and Round Top peaks.

As you approach the saddle, begin angling left, commencing a moderate climb to gain the ridge top, which you crest at 1.4 miles. Follow the ridge along its northwest pattern over mild terrain until you reach the base of the first of five peaks at 1.8 miles. Little Round Top is often obscured by the ridge and the other peaks, but the view to the southwest down on shapely Caples Lake, topped by Round Top east of it, is inspirational.

A brief but steep climb puts you atop the first peak, where those lacking time and/or energy can savor the panorama, which includes previously mentioned views along with Lake Tahoe, then head back. Pressing on, a brief drop and then another ascent, avoiding the obvious hanging cornices that sometimes form on the ridge edges, gets you to the top of Peak 9450 at 2.6 miles. The meadow encasing the Upper Truckee River is dramatic from here.

The obvious route follows this same pattern—brief ups and downs—to snag awesome peaks spaced about a mile apart. Peaks 9422 and 9325 are equally breathtaking to be on, and after making it this far, the approach to Little Round Top is a cinch by comparison. After 0.8 mile of level trudging and then a brief ascent, you've reached this aptly named peak at 5 miles.

The spectacular panorama that unfolds here offers several unobstructed photographic opportunities. The peaks of Sonora Pass way south join Caples Lake, Round Top, and Elephants Back in the same view. The mountains of Desolation Wilderness accompany a full view of Lake Tahoe to the north.

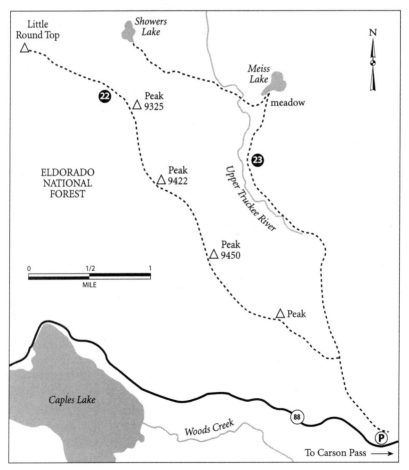

--23--

Upper Truckee River and Meiss Lake

Total distance: 7.4 miles
Hiking time: 5–7 hours
Difficulty: Moderate
Elevation gain: 1,000 feet
High point: 8,795 feet
Maps: USGS Caples Lake, USGS Carson Pass
Information: Amador Ranger District, Eldorado National Forest

Venture along the meandering course of the Upper Truckee River near where it originates, and if it's cold enough in the deep of winter, it may be a perfect sheet of ice. This narrow segment of river winds through a long and thin meadow to Meiss Lake, where, if snowpack is high, you may need a topo map to indicate whether you've reached it or if you're still in the meadow.

The scenery along the route is varied and inspirational. The first mile passes through an open forest to a saddle showing off handsome views of the Carson Pass mountains. You then descend into a gentle and expansive meadow that spans about 2 miles to the lake. To be ensconced in this pasture of white is to be surrounded by a plethora of smooth and rounded hillocks and smallish peaks, an uncommon high-country site that will be fondly etched in your memory.

If time and/or energy are lacking, consider getting to or near the saddle, savor your views of Caples Lake, Round Top, and Elephants Back across mostly bare terrain to the south, and then head back. Cross-country skiers sometimes take this route to Meiss Lake, but chances are still good you may have the place to yourself during weekdays. Ice fishing on the lake is occasionally relished by diehard fishermen/snowshoers.

From Carson Pass on Highway 88, drive 0.2 mile west and park on the north side of the highway in Meiss Meadow Sno-Park (see map on page 99). To obtain your pass, call (209) 258-7248.

Begin by heading west past a couple of hiking signs, generally contouring the lightly forested slopes. Grotesquely shaped, large specimens of Sierra juniper look even more peculiar interspersed with random colonies of quaking aspens that mingle with red fir and lodgepole pines. Bend your way into a modest drainage, then head for the obvious saddle to the north.

After admiring the views from the saddle at 1.2 miles, this journey's highest point, descend to the north through a slim drainage where sometimes cornices are present to the west hanging over the ridge crest. Just choose a descent course along the mountainside on the east of the drainage to avoid avalanche danger. Easy and rhythmic snowshoeing ensues upon entering the expansive meadow at 1.6 miles. Widely scattered, modest-sized conifers decorate the banks of the Upper Truckee River, with a scenic ridge featuring a series of evenly spaced, smallish promontories drawing raves to the west.

You make good time meadow trudging while lost in a refreshing daydream to the lake at 3.7 miles. Spot the lake at the northeast end of a large clearing, just in front of some low hills densely covered in lodgepole pines and red firs. Randomly scattered boulder slabs accentuate the shoreline. From the southwest end of Meiss Lake, you can easily trudge west by northwest over mostly level terrain for 1.2 miles to Showers Lake.

On the way to Meiss Lake

--24--

Red Lake Peak

Total distance: 5.6 miles
Hiking time: 4–7 hours
Difficulty: Moderate to strenuous
Elevation gain: 1,500 feet
High point: 10,063 feet
Maps: USGS Caples Lake, USGS Carson Pass
Information: Amador Ranger District, Eldorado National Forest

Lofty Red Lake Peak is the ideal perch for adoring wondrous Hope Valley as it sprawls from Thompson Peak to the north to just beyond Carson Pass to the south. Depending on the snowshoe season, Hope Valley can range from a huge meadow glistening in snow to spacious green fields sliced by the West Fork of the Carson River. Also from Red Lake Peak, Lake Tahoe is dramatic, bordered by snow-capped peaks in winter. The route climbs wide, open slopes most of the way, furnishing inspirational views throughout.

The pass west of Red Lake Peak

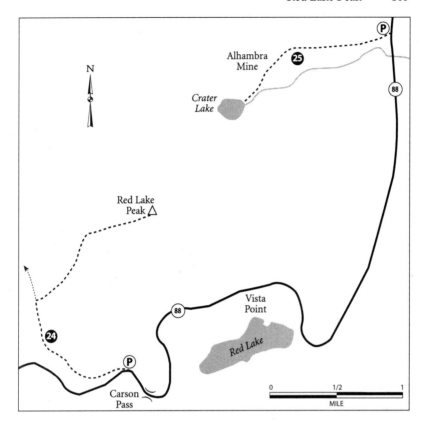

Red Lake Peak was the first Sierra mountain climbed by Caucasians, as well as being the vista point for the inaugural view of Lake Tahoe, which was recorded on February 14, 1844, by John C. Fremont.

Cross-country skiers sometimes exert themselves to the crest of Red Lake Peak for the thrill of the downhill return trip. This remote region is home to the elusive pine marten, a low-slung mammal with a bushy tail. Watch for a coyote downslope at the edge of the red fir forest. Look for hare and deer tracks in the snow.

From Carson Pass on Highway 88, drive 0.2 mile west and park on the north side of the highway in Meiss Meadow Sno-Park. To obtain your pass, call (209) 258-7248.

To start, head west, generally contouring the lightly forested slopes. Admire the grotesquely shaped, large specimens of Sierra juniper that mingle with red fir and lodgepole pines. Bend your way into a modest drainage, then head for the obvious saddle to the north, which you bag at 1.2 miles. The bare terrain offers awesome views to the south of Elephants Back and Round Top peaks.

Veer northeast and angle across moderately steep and wide, open slopes beneath towering Red Lake Peak. Curve just below the first rock outcropping on the ridge above, and soon you can plan your course up Red Lake Peak proper. Just head for the high point on the blunt ridge south of the boulders atop the true top.

It takes mountaineering equipment to get to the actual highest top of Red Lake Peak. But a next highest point is just a few feet lower in elevation and a mere stone's throw away. Besides, you've come this far and you're sweaty and out of breath and probably aren't the least concerned. The array of steep peaks and deep canyons in the Carson Pass area to the south are dramatic, including Round Top and Elephants Back. Hope Valley gets your attention to the east while Lake Tahoe highlights the northern view along with the Crystal Range. To the west, Little Round Top and a series of peaks that lead to it take center stage.

-- 25 --

Crater Lake

Total distance: 3 miles
Hiking time: 3–5 hours
Difficulty: Moderate to strenuous
Elevation gain: 1,300 feet
High point: 8,595 feet
Map: USGS Carson Pass
Information: Amador Ranger District, Eldorado National Forest

Crater Lake is tucked in a sensational cirque basin, offering dramatic views of Hope Valley and featuring ultra privacy. As you traipse undiscovered on the steep and direct route to this small circular lake, pause often to admire the sprawling Hope Valley, which can range from a huge meadow glistening in snow to vibrant and spacious green fields sliced by the West Fork of the Carson River, depending on the season. Find a statuesque conifer in the open forest to be in the foreground for a photo of the Carson Pass area to the south.

Like most snow-covered lakes, it's not easy to recognize the crystal clear water that lies beneath. With its eastern exposure, Crater Lake gets mainly the cool morning sun, and therefore holds snow longer in the season. The beauty

Hope Valley view from lip of Crater Lake

of this lake in winter and early spring is the steep rocky escarpments that surround it. From the usually shaded west side of the lake, a wandering soul can feel that nobody else was ever here. This is a place where a hibernating black bear might venture out briefly to stretch. It's a tranquil spot where the gray-crowned rosy finch flittering in the pines or the Steller's jay squawking in the shrubbery might be heard.

Because routefinding skills might be put into practice, and since the far-reaching views are such a highlight of the journey, choose a half-day of good weather to claim Crater Lake. Call ahead for the latest information on avalanche danger. Occasionally, cross-country skiers use the roads that zigzag up the slope.

To get there, drive Highway 88 to a spot 4.4 miles northeast of Carson Pass and 4.1 miles southwest of the Highway 88/89 junction. Park for free in the small plowed area on the west side of the highway (see map on page 103).

The trip begins on the lovely west edge of Hope Valley, in a large quaking aspen grove just north of Crater Lake's outlet creek. Follow the swift stream for 0.25 mile or so, than angle up the slope among the lodgepole pines, red firs, Jeffrey pines, and incense cedars. Locate massive Stevens Peak to the west by southwest, and stay just to the south of it as you climb moderately, due west. Aim for the low spot on the open ridge above as the conifer forest thins.

By 0.7 mile the climb intensifies, giving you a good excuse to stop to catch your breath and look back over the scenic Hope Valley. Toward the rocky lip that fronts the lake, the terrain gets even steeper, causing you to angle in the direction of the gentler slope along the creek. A few hundred feet of mellow trudging ensues before a final steep climb to the rim that promptly drops down to Crater Lake.

Plan on spending a lot of quality hang time exploring the lake, which is ruggedly encased by steep rock walls that are part of the flanks of Stevens Peak and Red Lake Peak (Route 24) to the southwest. From the lip of the basin, the cars look like marching ants and Sierra Nevada peaks abound to the east.

--26--
Scotts Lake and Waterhouse Peak

Total distance: 5–7.5 miles
Hiking time: 5–9 hours
Difficulty: Moderate to strenuous
Elevation gain: 2,200 feet
High point: 9,497 feet
Maps: USGS Freel Peak, USGS Echo Lake
Information: Lake Tahoe Basin Management Unit

A scenic meadow, a large pristine lake, and a challenging mountain—this remote route features all three, in that order. The majestic mountains of Carson Pass are viewed from Big Meadow, Scotts Lake, and Waterhouse Peak, all from a variety of unique and inviting vantage points (bring a lot of film).

If time, energy, and/or experience are in short supply, skip Waterhouse Peak. Its climb is relentless and particularly steep toward the top. Call ahead of time for potential avalanche danger, and choose a clear and windless day if you're aiming to claim the peak. The trek in the meadow to the lake is also suitable for cross-country skiers.

From the junction of Highways 89 and 50, drive south on 89 for 5.2 miles to the signed Big Meadow Trailhead. Go 150 yards farther, and park for free in the small lot on the left.

Lug your snowshoes down to the trailhead across the highway, then start climbing past Jeffrey pine, ponderosa pine, and red and white fir. Above aspen-lined Big Meadow Creek on the right, the trail weaves through the conifer forest on a fairly discernible route up the Big Meadow drainage. Lodgepole pine and quaking aspen flank a gate at 0.4 mile. Go right 75 yards farther at a signpost and promptly enter Big Meadow, which is surrounded by dense forest. Like all snowy meadows, Big Meadow is appropriate for beginning snowshoers and cross-country skiers to hone their skills in a beautiful and peaceful setting.

Trace the eastern border of Big Meadow Creek across the meadow for about 0.25 mile to where the creek forks, then dart left (east) into medium forest, heading up the Big Meadow Creek/Scotts Lake canyon. Stay well above the north bank of Big Meadow Creek because it's clogged with timber and willows. Keep climbing up the drainage in the deep forest, and eventually the grade eases as you approach the saddle. The forest thins here, and prominent views of Waterhouse Peak to the north get your attention.

At 2.3 miles, you reach the saddle proper, where views to the southwest of the imposing northeast face of Stevens Peak take center stage. Pear-shaped Scotts Lake lies invitingly just below the saddle at 2.5 miles. Your mission is to scurry down to it and then around it. From the north shore, the northeast face of Stevens Peak glares at you. This is where you make your big move to nab Waterhouse Peak.

Jeffrey pines and red firs accompany you halfway up the south face at 3.2 miles, then the views down on Scotts Lake improve noticeably as you pause frequently to catch your breath and look back on the scenes you've been to. Reach a small plateau that you cross to get to the base of the rocky summit. A short but steep climb puts you atop Waterhouse Peak at 3.7 miles. As you traipse among the boulders and squat conifers atop the peak, a dramatic panorama

Waterhouse Peak from Big Meadow

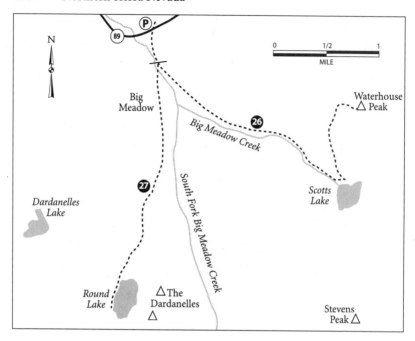

unfolds. Lake Tahoe and the Crystal Range highlight your view to the northwest, while northern Sierra Nevada stretch in all directions. There's a red-tailed-hawk's-eye view down on Hope Valley to the east, while the mountains surrounding Carson Pass attract attention to the south.

--27--

Big Meadow and Round Lake

Total distance: 5.6 miles
Hiking time: 5–7 hours
Difficulty: Moderate
Elevation gain: 800 feet
High point: 8,037 feet
Maps: USGS Freel Peak, USGS Echo Lake
Information: Lake Tahoe Basin Management Unit

Cradled under the imposing cliffs of the volcanic Dardanelles, snow-clad Round Lake is pure and rapturous in winter. It's a prime destination after snowshoeing

Big Meadow

through an expansive meadow where the Steller's jay squawks, then trudging through a forest where the great horned owl perches sneakily. As an added bonus, you get to scan the Upper Truckee River drainage on this remote route sometimes shared by cross-country skiers and dogs.

Pay close attention to the route just past the meadow to ensure you're headed in the direction of fittingly named Round Lake. It's best to go several days after a snowfall, with the hope someone has already set tracks to follow. Meiss Lake is a mere 1.2 miles south of Round Lake, and an ultimate 8-mile, one-way trip can be arranged with a car shuttle (Route 23).

From the junction of Highways 89 and 50, drive south on 89 for 5.2 miles to the signed Big Meadow trailhead. Go 150 yards farther, and park for free in the small lot on the left.

Carry your snowshoes down to the trailhead across the highway, then start climbing past Jeffrey pine, ponderosa pine, and red and white fir. Above aspen-lined Big Meadow Creek on the right, the trail weaves through the conifer forest on a fairly discernible route up the Big Meadow drainage. Lodgepole pine and quaking aspen flank a gate at 0.4 mile. Go right 75 yards farther at a signpost and promptly enter Big Meadow, which is surrounded by dense forest.

Carefully cross Big Meadow Creek and head west for the edge of forest and meadow. Tracing the meadow's western edge has two big benefits. It helps keep your feet dry if the snow pack is scant, and you're treated to ongoing views of dynamic Waterhouse Peak to the east. Like all snowy meadows, Big Meadow offers novice snowshoers the chance to rehearse their stride and technique.

After 0.4 mile's worth of gliding south along the meadow border, resume climbing in an open forest. The ascent intensifies as you approach a forested pinnacle 0.5 mile beyond Big Meadow. Pass below the pinnacle across the forested slopes on the east side of the ridge and climb to a pass separating the Upper Truckee River and Big Meadow Creek tributaries at 1.6 miles. Check out Waterhouse Peak here and Upper Truckee River territory to the west.

Angle down across the steep, forested slope to the bottom of the drainage. Negotiate your way up the main channel that drains Round Lake. Follow the creek and eventually get to a steep slope, where you descend the short length to Round Lake at 2.8 miles.

Plan to take the easy, shoreline stroll past sagebrush, Sierra juniper, western white pine, and lodgepole pine. The sheer rock walls of the Dardanelles to the immediate east create a dramatic backdrop to the scenic lake.

Fallen Leaf Lake and Mount Tallac

LAKE TAHOE AREA

From Highway 50 to Highway 80

--28--

Echo Lakes

Total distance: 2–8 miles
Hiking time: 2–6 hours
Difficulty: Easy
Elevation gain: 400 feet
High point: 7,525 feet
Map: USGS Echo Lake
Information: Eldorado National Forest

Oblong and surprisingly large, Echo Lakes transform from a major tourist attraction in the summer to a remote scene of peaceful and gleaming snow white in the winter and early spring. With easy-to-negotiate terrain, Echo Lakes are the southeast gateways to the spectacular Desolation Wilderness, meaning you might meet cross-country skiers, dogs, and other snowshoers of all levels.

Long, lakeside strolls tend to turn into refreshing, satisfying, daydreamy excursions, and this route fits that bill ideally. Merely follow a snow-covered road for about a mile, trudge the south shores of Lower Echo Lake and Upper Echo Lake until you've had your fill, and then head back. The rugged scenery is composed of sheer rocky cliffs of granite that rise steeply above the gleaming lakes.

This is a good trek to take when wet weather and big winds are coming in, because the exit is easy and the course is sure. Like any high mountain lake during snow season, wander out onto Echo Lakes only if there's a substantial snowpack on them, and even then, it's safer to explore near the edge. For sure, avoid the areas near the inlets and outlets, since they thaw faster.

From Highway 50's Echo Pass 12 miles southwest of South Lake Tahoe, drive west 0.8 mile, then turn right (north) on Johnson Pass Road. Follow the plowed road 0.5 mile, and park in Echo Lakes Sno-Park. Call (916) 324-1222 for locations that sell 1-day Sno-Park permits; otherwise, you'll have to park farther back on Johnson Pass Road or even off Highway 50 if there's too much snow, making sure your vehicle is well off either road.

Chances are the snow-covered road at the start will be packed from all kinds of tracks from all kinds of recreationists. Follow the alignment of Echo Lakes Road north, across from the Sno-Park. Your goal is to climb gently in a forest of red fir and Jeffrey pine to the first view of Lower Echo Lake at 1 mile. Scamper down past a scattered colony of alder shrubs to the shore and go with

Echo Lake

your temptation to stray to the spillway for superb views of the dock, hovering Becker Peak to the south (Route 29), and nearby Peak 7758 to the north.

Proceed around the south shore, alternating between staying low at the lake's edge for intimacy and going higher up for views. The south shores of both lakes feature a forest of Jeffrey pines and red firs with occasional clearings. It's these open spaces that you want to move to for the best views. Across the lake, the terrain is contrasting, with manzanita and huckleberry oak shrubs situated among boulder outcrops and Sierra junipers.

Roughly halfway up the length of Lower Echo Lake, at about 2.5 miles, there are improved views of Flagpole Peak rising 1,000 feet abruptly above Lower Echo Lake to the north, with Echo Peak also getting your attention to the northwest. You then negotiate around a long stretch of cabins, wondering if you could afford a week's stay in one. A bit less than 1 mile farther, scurry up to a vista point above Dartmouth Cove, which separates Lower Echo Lake from Upper Echo Lake. From this vantage point you'll note that the upper lake is nearly a clone of the lower lake, only it's about a third of its size. There's an

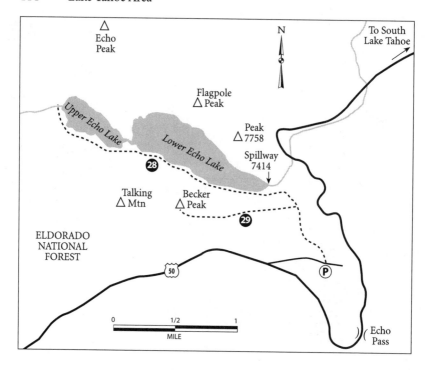

awesome view here of Pyramid Peak to the west, and other views of it are just as inspirational as you continue along all or part of Upper Echo Lake's south shore.

--*29*--

Becker Peak

Total distance: 3.4 miles
Hiking time: 3–5 hours
Difficulty: Moderate
Elevation gain: 1,100 feet
High point: 8,325 feet
Map: USGS Echo Lake
Information: Eldorado National Forest

Little-known Becker Peak is an ideally situated hub offering a vantage point for admiring several Desolation Wilderness place names from a refreshingly

Echo Lake from slope of Becker Peak

unique viewpoint. From this impressive conglomeration of big boulders, a snowshoer gets a red-tailed-hawk's-eye view straight down on gleaming Echo Lakes, which are usually snow-clad most of the winter and early spring. The layout of Crystal Range, neighbored by the stark visages of Echo Peak and Jacks Peak, makes Becker Peak a supreme spot for taking inspirational Sierra Nevada photos in the snow season. The best photos are usually taken by early afternoon.

The route is typically popular with cross-country skiers for the first part, but during the sudden climb of Becker Peak away from the snow tracks, you're more likely to see a coyote trotting along the slope or a porcupine nestled high in a conifer than a person.

From Highway 50's Echo Pass 12 miles southwest of South Lake Tahoe, drive west 0.8 mile, then turn right (north) on Johnson Pass Road. Follow the plowed road 0.5 mile, and park in Echo Lake's Sno-Park. Call (916) 324-1222 for locations that sell 1-day Sno-Park permits; otherwise, you'll have to park farther back on Johnson Pass Road or even off Highway 50 if there's too much snow, making sure your vehicle is well off either road.

Follow the alignment of Echo Lakes Road north, across from the Sno-Park. Your mission is to climb gently over the maze of tracks in a forest of red fir and Jeffrey pine to the first view down on the Echo Lakes at 1 mile. Veer left (west by southwest), and commence a slow trudge upslope. The grade eases when you gain the ridge after a couple hundred yards.

Mild ascent continues along the ridge in open forest for nearly 1 mile until you reach a rocky pinnacle.

Pass on the left and soon reach the steep slopes below Becker Peak. The final 150 feet of climbing to the tiptop are the toughest. The bumpy rocks tend to shed snow quickly, meaning that it might be best to shed your snowshoes while always choosing the safest and easiest way to the summit.

The views will keep you occupied a long while. The 8,824-foot-tall Talking Mountain dominates the western view, concealing most of Ralston Peak behind it. Talking Mountain is a mere 0.5 mile from Becker Peak along the ridge, and it warrants a visit if time and energy permit. Pyramid Peak, the Crystal Range, and Jacks Peak frame a view to the west by northwest, while Echo Peak takes center stage close by, across Echo Lakes. Freel Peak and a portion of Lake Tahoe to the east complete the panorama.

--30--
To Lookout

Angora Lookout and Angora Lakes

Total distance: 4–7.5 miles
Hiking time: 4–6 hours
Difficulty: Easy to moderate
Elevation gain: 900 feet
High point: 7,450 feet
Maps: USGS Emerald Bay, USGS Echo Lake
Information: Lake Tahoe Basin Management Unit

What a difference some snow makes. Experience firsthand the calm, wild, and remote Angora Lakes when decked out with pure white flakes, as opposed to summertime, when throngs of tourists guzzle sodas and sunbathe there. The panorama of powder-coated peaks and azure lakes atop Angora Lookout is a breathtaking treat, and having popular Angora Lakes all to yourself is special. The route is so straightforward—it climbs moderately on a road to the lookout and beyond—that cross-country skiers and occasional snowmobilers also enjoy the trip.

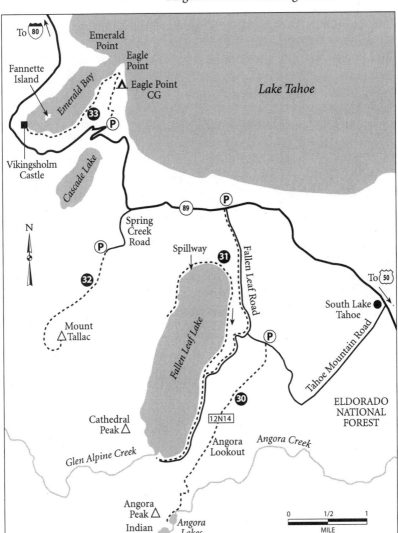

Directions

From the junction of Highways 50 and 89 in South Lake Tahoe, drive west on Lake Tahoe Boulevard 2.4 miles, then turn right onto Tahoe Mountain Road. Climb 1 mile and turn right onto Glenmore Way, followed immediately by a left onto Dundee Circle. Continue until you reach Tahoe Mountain Road again, then park for free near this intersection as space allows.

Descend along the road for about 150 yards to the start of Forest Service Road 12N14. Go left (south) into a pretty meadow lined with willows and

Fallen Leaf Lake and Angora Peak

quaking aspens. The road stays mostly straight for a while, in a peaceful mixed forest of ponderosa pine, Douglas fir, and incense cedar. Listen for the raucous chatter of the Steller's jay and the Douglas squirrel.

At 0.6 mile, the route climbs more noticeably, eventually reaching the crest of the ridge, where there are partial views of Mount Tallac and Angora Peak. Reach the lookout at 2 miles, where gorgeous views abound. Rectangular Fallen Leaf Lake nestles closely below to the northwest, topped by metamorphic Mount Tallac. A portion of Lake Tahoe embellishes your eastern view. Snowy and steep Ralston Peak dominates to the south. Tahoe Basin's highest peak, Freel Peak, stands tall to the southeast.

Continue southwest along the road from the lookout as it follows the gentle decline of the ridge crest, then angles around a knoll. The road then bends south and climbs steeply to the first of the Angora Lakes at 3.4 miles, where snowmobilers are not allowed. These likely frozen, matching gems are named for Angora goats once pastured here. They nestle in their rocky basins at the bottoms of steep cliffs that form the east face of 8,588-foot-high Angora Peak. To reach the nearby upper lake, head for the low notch through which a stream connects the upper and lower lakes. Private cabins ring the shoreline of both lakes, which are adorned with Jeffrey pine, Sierra juniper, lodgepole pine, mountain hemlock, pinemat manzanita, and huckleberry oak.

-- *31* --

Fallen Leaf Lake

Total distance: 3–10 miles
Hiking time: 2–5 hours
Difficulty: Easy
Elevation gain: 300 feet
High point: 6,550
Map: USGS Emerald Bay
Information: Lake Tahoe Basin Management Unit

Wandering along large Fallen Leaf Lake is an intimate, relaxing experience, one full of fantastic views of mighty Mount Tallac and photogenic Angora Peak. Cross-country skiers, weekend snowmobilers, and even hikers in boots congregate around the eastern shore, but you only have to venture westward a mile or so along the southern shore to attain deep peace and tranquility. Adventurous souls can negotiate the inlet crossing and circumnavigate the entire lake, just call ahead to check on avalanche danger on the southwestern banks of the lake. Keep in mind, though, the best views are seen from the water's southern edge.

Fallen Leaf Lake is ringed with conifers and features several tiny, pebbly beaches, some decorated with driftwood. Your mission is to explore as many of these nifty paradises as possible, searching for ducks that cruise the often choppy, azure lake, which generally does not freeze over. This oblong lake is second only to Lake Tahoe in size in the immediate Lake Tahoe vicinity.

From the Y road junction in South Lake Tahoe, drive north on Highway 89 for 2.8 miles to signed Fallen Leaf Road. Park for free in one of several tiny clearings on the side of Fallen Leaf Road or Highway 89. If there's too much snow to find safe parking way off the road, you must drive 0.5 mile farther and park in the large lot at Taylor Creek Sno-Park (see map on page 117). Call (916) 324-1222 to purchase a pass.

To start, head south for a bit over 1 mile to the lake, whether you're following Fallen Leaf Road or the marked trails at the Sno-park. Gain the shore, follow it west, and gather in the highlights. The snow-capped, metamorphic Mount Tallac is your constant visual companion to the northwest, while angular Angora Peak to the west will be spotted primarily from the various, alder-lined pocket beaches.

Make note of the quaking aspen-dotted meadow just to the south of Fallen

Leaf Lake—it's a nice spot to visit for a final snack on the way back. The best way to be sure you notice it is to traipse up the tree-clad hillside after about 200 yards of snowshoeing from the southeast corner of the lake.

Hug the banks of the lake, heading west beneath stately incense cedars, ponderosa pines, and Douglas firs. Open spots are often adorned with manzanita, gooseberry, and sagebrush. Even out of leaf, the limbs of the willow colonies along the far north shore are cheerful. Occasionally, you will pass various empty cabins and piles of firewood, hints of upcoming summer activity. Some of the petite beach strips feature colorful, shiny, and smooth pebbles that descend into the lake, where they are even brighter and more impressive.

At 5.5 miles reach rocky and attractive Glen Alpine Creek and the far southern edge of the lake. Although crossing here and totally encircling the lake is doable and adds variety to the route, I recommend more or less retracing your tracks and revisiting those inspirational views of Mount Tallac and neighboring Cathedral Peak.

--32--
Mount Tallac

Total distance: 5 miles
Hiking time: 7–11 hours
Difficulty: Strenuous
Elevation gain: 3,300 feet
High point: 9,735 feet
Map: USGS Emerald Bay
Information: Lake Tahoe Basin Management Unit

Climb mighty Mount Tallac when it's snow-clad, and you'll be sitting on top of a special world, one with hawk's-eye views down on Lake Tahoe Basin's most spectacular scenery. After all the sweat equity and grunting involved with trudging gradually up its northeast face, you'll be gasping and gawking at everything from Lake Tahoe and Fallen Leaf Lake to Ralston, Angora, and Echo Peaks.

For most snowshoers, Mount Tallac is the area's cardinal peak, and getting to the top is the region's premier achievement. But only advanced snowshoers, fit folks, and crazed souls should sign up. For starters, Mount Tallac is infamous for avalanche danger on its high-angle slopes (call ahead for a

Mount Tallac and Fallen Leaf Lake

report) and lightning during thunderstorms (don't get caught atop the peak in one). Second, the route's constantly steep rise straight up the mountain is not for the faint of heart. Be prepared to ask yourself during the journey why you talked yourself into this arduous ascent.

If you snowboard, the 3,300-foot thrill ride back down the mountain blows away anything you could get from a ski lift.

Drive north on Highway 89, 4.3 miles from its junction with Highway 50 in South Lake Tahoe. Turn west onto signed Spring Creek Road, go 0.6 mile to Pomo Road (also called Forest Road 1396), and then turn right. Follow this road 0.3 mile to its end and park for free on the side of the road (see map on page 117).

Break out of the trees and snowshoe toward the open gully as you ascend, halting periodically to catch your breath while admiring Lake Tahoe. After about 1,000 feet worth of steady climbing past widely scattered red firs, lodgepole pines, and manzanita, the grade eases as you enter a bowl. Keep climbing past the bowl, angling slightly southwest, arcing toward the north ridge. At

1.5 miles, reach the crest, where, if it's getting late or foul weather's coming in fast, you can absorb the great views and then boogie back down.

Our route switches south and dips to a saddle. Pick and choose your way up and around the ridge, then climb to the summit via the back side. Even in deep snow, there's bound to be a lot of rust- and orange-colored metamorphic boulders to sit on so you can gaze at the scenery.

To the west, much of the mostly granitic Desolation Wilderness, highlighted by Pyramid Peak, Crystal Range, and numerous lakes (some may be snow-free) take center stage. To the east, most of 1,645-foot-deep Lake Tahoe graces your view, capped by Freel Peak, Jobs Sister, and Mount Rose, the three tallest peaks in the Tahoe Basin, in that order. Rugged and rocky Angora Peak is breathtaking nearby to the south, with Echo and Becker Peaks in the same view, farther away. Plan on taking a couple of hours if time permits to wander over Mount Tallac, which is Washoe Indian for "great mountain."

-- ♪♪ --

Eagle Point and Emerald Bay

Total distance: 2–4 miles
Hiking time: 2–5 hours
Difficulty: Easy to moderate
Elevation gain: 400 feet
High point: 6,600 feet
Map: USGS Emerald Bay
Information: Emerald Bay State Park

Spy on a huge bald eagle's nest, glide over a pristine beach, admire staggering views of Mount Tallac, and capture the shiny blue essence of Emerald Bay on this remote ramble. You'll also get close enough to Lake Tahoe to skip a stone over it and close enough to Emerald Bay's Fannette Island to heave a rock toward it. A prime goal of this route is to locate the gray, twiggy eagle's nest, which is frequently visited by ospreys. It stands high over Emerald Bay, atop a long dead Jeffrey pine easily seen from aptly named and readily accessible Eagle Point.

From the junction of Highways 28 and 89, drive Highway 89 south for 20 miles to the large, paved turnout indicating Eagle Point Campground above

Emerald Bay and park for free. From the Highway 50 junction with Highway 89, travel north on Highway 89 for 9 miles.

Follow the Eagle Point Campground road, which winds downward for 1 mile (see map on page 117). It's a pleasant, scenic, and peaceful journey in a mixed forest of Jeffrey pine, white fir, and incense cedar. When you reach the road loop at 0.7 mile, head right and go counterclockwise. Spot campsite number 56 and take the short spur trail, which promptly reaches Eagle Point past thickets of manzanita and huckleberry oak shrubs.

Emerald Bay from Eagle Point

From the picnic table, you can see most of Lake Tahoe, with the yard-wide eagle's nest about 50 yards away centered in the view. Because of constant ripple action, Lake Tahoe never freezes over. Come on a sunny day, and Lake Tahoe and Emerald Bay are as deep blue and clear as can be. When you get to the beach at Emerald Bay, toss a white stone into the deep water. You may be able to watch it sink for up to 25 yards. The thin, clear mountain air allows the pure, crystalline water of lake and bay to reflect the blue sky above. It can also appear reddish during colorful sunsets or gray-black during storms. At 6,225 feet above sea level, Lake Tahoe is the highest lake of its size (22 miles long) in the United States. Its deepest point is 1,636 feet, making it the third-deepest lake in North America.

Double-back to the campground road and continue to a service road at campsite number 87. Take it down to Emerald Bay Beach, where a grand view of metamorphic Mount Tallac to the west awaits. Wander eastward several yards so you can dip your hand into the actual lake. Follow the shoreline west for about 1 mile to Vikingsholm Castle and Vikingsholm Beach for superb, close-up views of Fannette Island adorning Emerald Bay. Retrace your snowshoe prints back to campsite 87, then make the 1-mile-long trudge back to the trailhead.

-- 34 --

Meeks Creek

Total distance: 3.8 miles
Hiking time: 2–4 hours
Difficulty: Easy
Elevation gain: 200 feet
High point: 6,350 feet
Maps: USGS Homewood, USGS Meeks Bay
Information: Lake Tahoe Basin Management Unit

Here's a quick and easy way to attain deep peace, visit a pure and clear creek, and perhaps spot some wildlife. With several better-known routes nearby, Meeks Creek is saved for adventurous souls and/or beginning snowshoers who crave a solitary and satisfying wilderness experience. With tall conifers, scenic shrubbery, and a swift creek included in the journey, you're apt to see Steller's

Quaking aspens

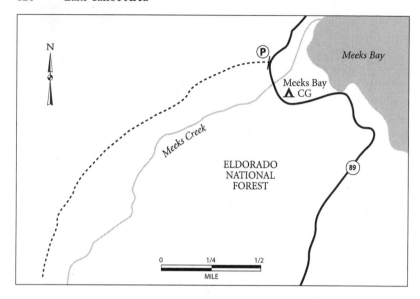

jays, red-tailed hawks, and mountain chickadees in the open forest and perhaps a great horned owl in the deeper woods.

Occasionally used by cross-country skiers and even hikers with boots, this route features flat terrain and simple routefinding, making it ideal after a huge batch of fresh powder has fallen or even during inclement weather. If snow is too skimpy here, you may have to move to a nearby higher elevation route described in this book. If you come in early spring, the creek is noisy and active and the willow buds swell.

From Highway 89 in Tahoe City, drive south for 11.2 miles and park for free in a lot on the west shoulder of the highway near a Forest Service signboard.

Trudge southwest following the course of snow-covered Forest Road 14N32. As you head gently up the broad and smooth valley, scan the willow-lined, meandering meadow to the south that encases Meeks Creek. The mostly flat open forest border you're in is composed of incense cedars, ponderosa pines, white firs, lodgepole pines, and sporadic clusters of manzanita. An unnamed mountain with a top that resembles a nipple graces your view across meadow strips to the south.

At the far end of the meadows, you enter a dense stand of cool forest and then the road terminates at 1.6 miles. The goal here is to either safely cross Meeks Creek and follow its curving course back to the trailhead at Highway 89 (round trip of 3.8 miles) or trace the north banks of the creek for a while, then cut across the meadow and regain the Forest Road.

-- *35* --

Blackwood Canyon to Barker Pass

Total distance: 14 miles
Hiking time: 9 hours–2 days
Difficulty: Moderate
Elevation gain: 1,200 feet
High point: 7,280 feet
Map: USGS Homewood
Information: Lake Tahoe Basin Management Unit

Visit a large grove of quaking aspens, explore scenic Blackwood Creek, and earn Barker Pass, which offers grand views of Tahoe area peaks. The easy-to-negotiate route follows an old, snow-covered road, which often has a surprising number of animal tracks crossing it, including predators such as coyote and long-tailed weasel. Look for porcupines feeding high in the conifers or red-tailed hawks patrolling from high above.

Quaking aspens along Blackwood Creek

You may encounter cross-country skiers any day of the week on this popular route, and sometimes snowmobilers show up on weekends. Because the first couple of miles are level and the snow-covered road is easy to follow, this trip can be abbreviated when inclement weather hits, still making for a satisfying outing. If you roam from the trail, avoid the steeper terrain on the south side of Blackwood Canyon because of the avalanche danger.

Head south on Highway 89 for 4.1 miles from its junction with Highway 28 in Tahoe City. Turn west into the signed Blackwood Canyon Sno-Park. Call (530) 573-2600 to purchase a pass.

Start following the wide route as it heads west on an easy grade. After 0.4 mile, veer left into the lovely quaking aspen grove alongside Blackwood Creek. These deciduous trees related to the cottonwood feature stylish, grayish-white trunks. These trees reproduced through root suckering, creating groups of genetically identical clones. The northern flicker and house wren often flutter about in these trees and the neighboring orange-limbed willows.

Back on the main trail, a head-on view of Twin Peaks is nice. The climb is barely noticeable in a forest of white fir, Douglas fir, lodgepole pine, and tall and handsome ponderosa pine. At 2.5 miles, ignore a less obvious road and follow the route to the left over serpentine-bottomed Blackwood Creek. Those short on time and/or energy will find this picnic spot a good turnaround point and destination.

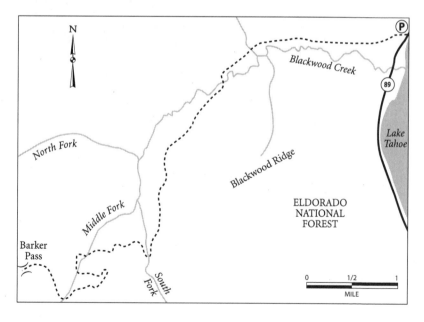

Pressing on, climbing becomes moderate on the other side of the canyon as the road bends southwest and heads up and away from the canyon bottom. Improved views of nearby unnamed ridges and peaks reward your steady efforts. The road crosses over the South Fork of Blackwood Creek at 4.6 miles. Note that the crowds of folks are long gone.

The ensuing 2.5 miles wander upward, deep into the wild and serene forest, with little scenery change until the views open up atop Barker Pass. The white firs and ponderosa pines are gradually replaced with red firs and Jeffrey pines along the steep ascent.

--*36*--

Loch Leven Lakes

Total distance: 7.4 miles
Hiking time: 5–8 hours
Difficulty: Moderate to strenuous
Elevation gain: 1,500 feet
High point: 6,850 feet
Maps: USGS Soda Springs, USGS Cisco Grove
Information: Nevada City Ranger District, Tahoe National Forest

Seek the curvaceous shorelines of three granite-ringed, high-mountain lakes and delight in each lake's special granitic islands. The photo opportunities are there—vistas of valleys and snowy ridges, glaciated mountain terrain, powdery alpine meadows, and pristine lakes. Ah, but there is a price and a tradeoff. The first 2 miles climb incessantly (1,300 feet of elevation gain); and you'll see and hear I-80 traffic over that span. The payoff happens when you're gliding across untouched snow at the trio of Loch Leven Lakes without a trace of civilization. This journey requires some careful routefinding skills. There's a good chance the snow line is a bit higher up, meaning you may have to lug your snowshoes for a ways, but you'll have a path to follow. This is also a good snowshoe route lasting perhaps into early May.

From I-80 (some 75 miles east of Sacramento), take the Cisco Grove exit and bear right onto Hampshire Rocks Road. Drive east for 2 miles, then park in the large paved lot for free.

The signed trail proceeds in a Jeffrey and lodgepole pine open forest sprinkled with numerous granite outcrops deposited by receding glaciers.

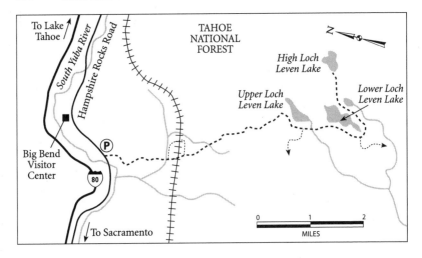

Chances are you're cutting virgin tracks, so proceed generally south on a course that loses the least amount of elevation on the far side. You may pass a pond at 0.7 mile, then continue climbing just to the east of a hillside covered by deciduous red cherry shrubs.

Cross an alder- and dogwood-lined creek that feeds into the South Yuba River below, soon cross railroad tracks at 1.4 miles, and then resume the uphill push as western white pine and the occasional quaking aspen join the mostly dense forest cover. Bear just to the right of some steep and bare cliffs, making a steady climb southeast toward the ridge top. Catch your breath and look north for good views down on the South Yuba River. The way finally levels at 2.4 miles and passes through a red fir forest before a brief descent to Upper Loch Leven Lake at 2.9 miles.

Surrounded by lodgepole pine (two needles to a bunch) and western white pines (five needles to a cluster), Upper Loch Leven Lake's shoreline is also laced with granite outcrops. Much larger Lower Loch Leven Lake at 3.3 miles is prettier than its nearby cousin. The route traces this lovely lake for 0.3 mile through huckleberry oak and mountain spiraea, both smashed by winter and spring snow.

Bear left at the slender southern tip of the lake at 3.7 miles, then ascend moderately the last 0.5 mile while admiring good views of grayish-brown Snow Mountain to the southeast. High Loch Leven Lake is the most secluded and arguably the most beautiful of the three lakes. The granite slabs look like gigantic pillows when snow-covered, and they surround most of the tiny island-dotted waters, while red fir, white pine, and lodgepole pine furnish shoreline shade for the south side campsites.

-- 37 --

Donner Pass to Mount Judah

Total distance: 5 miles
Hiking time: 4–5 hours
Difficulty: Moderate
Elevation gain: 1,300 feet
High point: 8,243 feet
Map: USGS Norden
Information: Tahoe National Forest

Linger atop two notable peaks offering exquisite views of Donner Lake and high Sierra Nevada in an area laden with history. This is the land of the ill-fated Donner Party of 1847's extraordinarily snowy winter. Donner Pass was also the travel corridor of the Washoe Indians, who carried pine nuts and obsidian to trade with the Euro-Americans. Nearly 300,000 people crossed the Sierra Nevada by wagon via Donner Pass, and the historic railroad still runs across the slopes of Donner Peak.

Steep domes and spires of sheer granite dominate the region, which you might share with rock climbers, dogs, and even snowboarders. The mostly open and rocky terrain is fairly steep but negotiable with careful picking and choosing of your route (always take the easiest and safest). You'll enjoy a long respite from climbing atop the gentle, protracted crest leading to Mount Judah's summit.

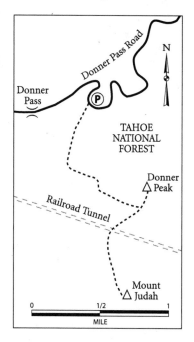

From Highway 80 just west of the junction with Highway 89 near Truckee, take the scenic and old Donner Pass Road about 3 miles up to Donner Pass. Park for free in the Donner Pass Observation Point paved lot next to the interpretive signs and metal railing. Watching for cars, carry your snowshoes across and then west on the road for a couple hundred yards until you spot a good route southeast up Donner Peak.

Donner Lake from slope of Donner Peak

Head up the moderately steep mountainside of the northwest slope of Donner Peak past widely scattered lodgepole pine, red fir, and Jeffrey pine. Thick-trunked specimens of Sierra juniper trees are picturesque poking above granite slabs. The initial views are west of attractive Lake Van Norden and the unnamed peaks above Donner Pass to the north. At 0.6 mile, reach the crest of Peak 7696, where a panorama featuring beach-lined and conifer-ringed Donner Lake awaits.

Continuing the ascent, pass through a stand of conifers before reaching the saddle that separates Donner Peak from Mount Judah at 1 mile. Turn northeast and trudge briefly up to the summit rocks of Donner Peak. Stare at the massive cornices that loom above Mount Judah's ridge and the array of peaks spreading north to south. Sky blue like Lake Tahoe on sunny days and light black on cloudy days, spacious Donner Lake deserves attention to the east. Look for cascades streaming over granite blocks here and off in the distance.

Retrace your snowshoe prints back to the saddle, then climb steeply up the slope toward the long summit ridge of Mount Judah. Once on the crest at 2 miles, the grade eases noticeably, as you head for the true summit at the south end. Be sure to avoid the cornices on the west edge as you readily gain the summit. The panorama here rivals Donner Peak and point 7696, only with differing rock outcrops and conifer specimens in the foreground, plus sightings of skiers careening down the ski slopes of Donner Ski Ranch and Sugar Bowl. You're also apt to see trains chugging across Donner Pass below. A wild scene occurs to the south, where a parade of snow-clad peaks marches along a series of steep ridges.

-- *38* --

Andesite Peak

Total distance: 3.6 miles
Hiking time: 3–5 hours
Difficulty: Moderate
Elevation gain: 1,000 feet
High point: 8,219 feet
Map: USGS Norden
Information: Tahoe National Forest

Little-known Andesite Peak is a snowshoer's paradise, featuring solitude and superb views of the northern realm of the Lake Tahoe region. Your photos are

Andesite Peak

likely to turn out just as good as those taken atop nearby Castle Peak (Route 40), which demands another 3 miles of hiking and 900 vertical feet to attain.

With the route's remoteness and mix of conifers and rocky crevices, you're more apt to spot wildlife. Look for porcupines feeding high in the tree cavities or pine marten tracks in the snow. If it's early spring, you may see the bushy-tailed wood rat or Douglas squirrel. The gray-crowned rosy finch frequently flitters in the pines.

From I-80 just west of Donner Summit, take the Castle Peak exit. Drive under the freeway to the north side of the westbound off-ramp, find a clearing along the road that heads upward to the northeast, and park for free. If there's too much snow or too many cars here, you must then go back under the freeway and follow signs to the nearby Sno-Park. Call (916) 324-1222 to purchase a pass.

Although steep in spots, the route is easy to negotiate—just gain the ridge and follow it to the top. The easiest method is to begin climbing the snow-covered road in a medium forest of red fir and lodgepole pine. At the southern edge of Castle Valley at 0.3 mile, veer sharply left (west) and promptly spot a rocky promontory that resembles a rook in a chess game. This is Peak 7605, which forms the southern flank of Andesite Ridge. It's well worth getting to

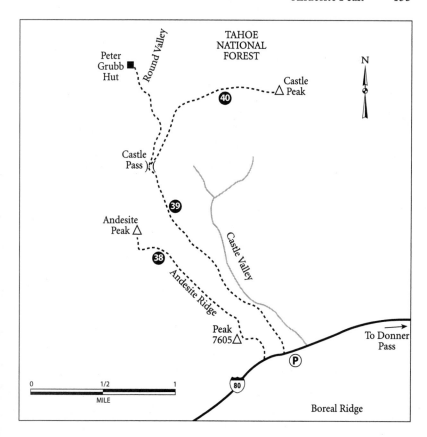

the top—just angle around the west side, then make the final strides on the northwest side. Unique views of Castle Peak and North Tahoe mountains to the east, and Boreal Ridge to the south, await. Peak 7605's crest is a conglomerate of bumpy rock etched with lichens.

The grade eases considerably as you trudge northwest along mostly open Andesite Ridge with inspiring views of Donner Summit behind you and Castle Peak to the east. Moderate forest cover returns along with a final burst of steep climbing at the base of Andesite Peak at 1.4 miles. Watch for and avoid large cornices on the eastern end of the peak, often formed by prevailing westerly winds. The terrain becomes gentle again just before reaching the broad summit of Andesite Peak at 1.7 miles.

From the top, extensive Sand Ridge to the north seems almost close enough to hurl a snowball toward. The spacious top of Andesite Peak is littered with small conifers that look like weird snowmen after a snowfall.

-- *39* --

Castle Valley to Round Valley

Total distance: 5.5 miles
Hiking time: 3–5 hours
Difficulty: Easy
Elevation gain: 700 feet
High point: 7,900 feet
Map: USGS Norden
Information: Tahoe National Forest

Fittingly named Round Valley and Castle Valley undergo a major transformation when blessed with pure white snow in the winter, which usually lasts through mid-spring. What was typical and blasé in the summer becomes soft and scenic, a pleasure in the white season. The ease of the route and the nice mix of small and tall conifers, sometimes draped lovingly with powder, allows a soul to aimlessly daydream to the simple rhythm of the snowshoes.

Rectangular Castle Peak, resembling a huge white molar, looms above you to the east the whole way, giving reason to crane your head often to get your view fix. Stylish Peter Grubb Hut makes for a fine destination, and you can stay overnight by contacting the Sierra Club at (530) 426-3632. This way there's plenty of time to climb Castle Peak (Route 40) or explore the wild backcountry to the north to obtain the solitude that may be lacking on the popular trip to the hut. For more aloneness and ease of parking, do this route on a weekday.

From I-80 just west of Donner Summit, take the Castle Peak exit. Drive under the freeway to the north side of the westbound off-ramp, find a clearing along the road that heads upward to the northeast, and park for free (see map on page 135). If there's too much snow or too many cars here, you must then go back under the freeway and follow signs to the nearby Sno-Park. Call (916) 324-1222 to purchase a pass.

Begin climbing the snow-covered road in a medium forest of red fir and lodgepole pine. Reach spacious Castle Valley at 0.4 mile and note the tiny lodgepole pines that dot this mellow meadow. Admire the stark face of Castle Peak as you traipse along the western edge of the meadow, staying just above it most of the way. Simply follow the tracks of previous snowshoers, staying to the side of the cross-country ski tracks. Otherwise, periodically placed blue markers guide the route.

Sierra juniper

Gradually depart the meadow as you head into moderate forest cover and commence a mild climb. The grade increases noticeably toward the head of the canyon, but soon you've claimed Castle Pass at 2 miles, where views spanning Castle Valley and up to Castle Peak to the east take center stage. The ski runs of Sugar Bowl, Boreal Ridge, and Northstar carpet the mountainsides near Donner Summit to the south.

Continue along the ridge northeast toward Castle Peak for a while, and soon descend mildly through light fir forest for 0.4 mile to the edge of a hill overlooking peaceful Round Valley. Make your way down to the hut and the gentle, open slopes of Round Valley. Surrounded by red firs, Peter Grubb Hut is an A-frame made of stone and wood with a ladder that leads to the upper loft. Round Valley invites you to head into the middle of it for a picnic and sightseeing.

--40--

Castle Peak

Total distance: 6.6 miles
Hiking time: 5–9 hours
Difficulty: Strenuous
Elevation gain: 1,900 feet
High point: 9,100
Map: USGS Norden
Information: Tahoe National Forest

Mostly flat-topped, chunky-looking Castle Peak is wild and remote country, where a snowshoeing soul can savor top-of-the-world views and spend quality hang time exploring this extensive summit. This route takes you past conifers into a broad and open valley, up to a forested pass, and then along an exposed and rocky ridge that reveals countless views of Tahoe and Donner Summit mountains.

You may see cross-country skiers and dogs in the valley, but you are likely to have Castle Peak's slopes to yourself. Only rarely will you see a snowshoer or careening snowboarder in the higher reaches. Box-shaped Castle Peak, looking like a mammoth white molar, graces the scene to the east the first half of the way, giving reason to crane your head often to size up the challenge. For more aloneness and ease of parking, do this route on a weekday.

Castle Peak

From I-80 just west of Donner Summit, take the Castle Peak exit. Drive under the freeway to the north side of the westbound off-ramp, find a clearing along the road that heads upward to the northeast, and park for free (see map on page 135). If there's too much snow or too many cars here, you must then go back under the freeway and follow signs to the nearby Sno-Park. Call (916) 324-1222 to purchase a pass.

Start climbing the snow-covered road in a light forest of red fir and lodgepole pine. Enter roomy Castle Valley at 0.4 mile where smallish lodgepole pines dot the mellow meadow. The stark face of Castle Peak stays visible as you trudge mostly above the western edge of the meadow. Simply follow the tracks of previous snowshoers, staying to the side of the cross-country ski tracks. Otherwise, periodically placed blue markers guide the route.

Gradually leave the valley as you climb mildly in medium forest. The grade increases toward the head of the canyon, and soon you've reached Castle Pass at 2 miles, where views spanning Castle Valley and up to Castle Peak to the east take center stage. The ski runs of Sugar Bowl, Boreal Ridge, and Northstar carpet the mountainsides near Donner Summit to the south.

Views continually improve as you head up the west ridge of Castle Peak while the trees get smaller and sparser. Higher up the slope, negotiate the safest, least-steep, and easiest route, then turn southeast toward the crest at 3 miles for the few hundred yards to the tippy top of Castle Peak. As you stroll around the spacious summit, previously mentioned views are now joined by rows of the Sierra Buttes and Desolation Wilderness peaks.

Lake Helen and Mount Diller

LASSEN VOLCANIC NATIONAL PARK AREA

Highway 36 to Highway 44

--*41*--

Susan River

Total distance: 13 miles; 6 miles with car shuttle
Hiking time: 4–8 hours
Difficulty: Easy
Elevation gain: 500 feet
High point: 4,660 feet
Maps: USGS Susanville, USGS Roop Mountain.
Information: Eagle Lake Resource Area, Bureau of Land Management

The Bizz Johnson Trail is an abandoned railroad line that provides a comfortable way to explore up close and personal a scenic stretch of the Susan River before it empties into large Honey Lake. Thanks to legendary outdoorsman John Reginato's idea and the Bureau of Land Management's work, the route that traces the Lassen and Fernley railroad lines was converted into a 30-mile-long trail. This snowshoe route covers the eastern portion, reaching Devils Corral just off Highway 36, which has a trailhead 7 miles west of Susanville that can shorten this hike to less than half the distance if a car shuttle is arranged.

You're apt to see a few fishermen or Lassen College students cross-country skiing along the wide and level path. Even when it's snowing, this route that traces the banks of the meandering Susan River is a cinch to follow. Because of the low elevation, it's best to call ahead to determine if there is enough snow for snowshoeing.

Drive to Susanville, which is on Highway 36 East and a few miles north of the end of Highway 395. Turn south on Weatherlow Street, which soon becomes Richmond Road. After 0.5 mile, park for free across from the historic Susanville Railroad Depot.

Consider the first mile a warm-up as you pass behind a neighborhood before crossing a rustic metal bridge above a lazy part of the Susan River. Vertical, jagged cliffs of sheer rock are like a shrine towering over the scene. This part and most of the trip reveal a stark contrast of dry slopes and moist banks. Bitterbrush and sagebrush eke existences between lichen-coated lava rocks, while willows and magnificently mature black cottonwoods clog the riverbanks. Black oaks, western junipers, and elderberry are interspersed.

Cross an oil-stained wooden bridge at 1.5 miles, overlooking gravel bar

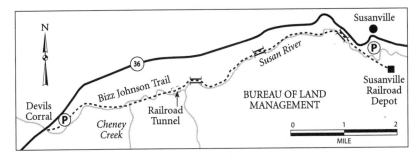

islands situated in the river. A forest of ponderosa pine decorates beyond the far shore (now to your left), while occasional and shorter ponderosa pine specimens join scattered black oaks on the mostly barren slope to the right.

The mostly exposed route reaches a couple of spur trails with easy access to the creek (now hugging trailside) and a well-placed bench at 2.1 miles. Folks tend to get more scarce from here on out as you get into the really good stuff—pristine and wild country that gets whisper-quiet at times, save for the chirping of the birds or the passage of modest rapids. Perhaps the best and deepest swimming hole on this journey appears below a wood and concrete bridge at 2.8 miles. Note the wonderfully sloped and rugged canyonsides at the next bridge 150 yards farther. It's nature's ideal mix of ponderosa pines above a black cottonwood grove, with random basalt boulder piles and a mosaic of chaparral shrubs. Look for the gorgeous seasonal stream 200 yards farther that cascades down the gentle north slope next to a dramatic basaltic outcrop. These big boulders resemble huge, fluffy pillows after a new snow.

A conifer-clad peak stands guard over an unnamed stream that finishes into the river. A nice campsite sets on the far shore at 3.8 miles. Conifers begin shading creek sections, contrasting nicely with bright willows and the stalwart limbs of large cottonwoods.

For the first time on the journey, the Bizz Johnson Trail rises well above the river, interrupted on its course by closet-sized boulders. Cross another wooden bridge next to a marshy strip of the river at 4.8 miles and then spend some hang time in a railroad tunnel, which is naturally air-conditioned year-round. Built in 1914, this dark and echoey tunnel allowed trains to pass through to service the timber industry. Builders had the dangerous task of blasting through solid rock to carve out this 150-yard-long tunnel.

Once through, peer behind you to admire the conglomerate of rocks forming a cliff and encasing this passageway. The next 1.5 miles or so feature more of the previously described highlights, including a slender but long meadow strip, several deep holes, and more jumbles of lava rock.

--42--

Lake Almanor Recreation Trail

Total distance: Up to 11 miles
Hiking time: 3–7 hours
Difficulty: Easy
Elevation gain: 300 feet
High point: 4,600 feet
Map: Lassen National Forest winter guide map
Information: Lassen National Forest, Almanor Ranger District

It's new, different, mellow, scenic, and virtually people-free during the snow season. The extraordinary Lake Almanor Recreation Trail may serve walkers, cyclists, and dogs from mid-spring through fall, but the route is custom-made for snowshoers and cross-country skiers when there's snow.

Snow covers a paved, 10-foot-wide path that escorts you through peaceful tall forests and along western edges of extra-large Lake Almanor, truly one of

Lake Almanor's snow melts quickly in the full sun

Lassen National Forest's ultimate lake gems. Spectacular views of Dyer Mountain, Lake Almanor, and many snow-clad high peaks in Lassen Volcanic National Park await.

Created in 1914 as a hydroelectric facility by the long-defunct Great Western Power Company, the lake rests at an elevation of 4,500 feet, spans 13 miles long, and extends 6 miles wide. The name Almanor originated by combining the names of three sisters—Alice, Martha, and Elinore—daughters of the power company's vice president. The dam was later built in 1927.

The easy-to-follow route may not have enough snow for snowshoeing, so check ahead. If not, consider higher elevation routes nearby, including Route 43 (Nanny Creek), Route 45 (Lake Helen), or Route 46 (Cinder Cone). Bring your pole for winter fishing the azure waters of Lake Almanor, which is 90 feet deep at its deepest point. This is one of those routes where you can do the whole thing or turn back any time you wish.

From the junction of Highways 89 and 36 just west of the town of Chester, turn south on Highway 89. When you reach the sign for Humbug Road after 4.6 miles, turn left, drive 75 yards to the signed trailhead, and park for free.

At the start, easy trudging occurs beneath stately ponderosa pines with occasional large specimens of white firs. Greenleaf manzanita pokes through the snow. After less than 1 mile, enter one of many small meadows that grace this gently rolling route. Look for osprey, bald eagles, and black-tailed deer. Watch for an eagle perched in a tree, waiting to sight and then dive on prey on the ground. Osprey hunt in the air, hovering for several seconds before

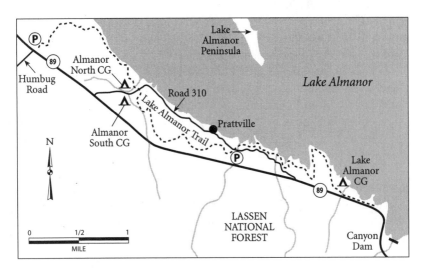

plunging. Your inaugural encounter with lake's edge, the first of many, happens after 1 mile, where you're greeted with a nice view east, across the lake of hogback-shaped Dyer Mountain.

Enjoy the lake's edge for nearly 1 mile, and if snow has receded enough, marvel at the profusion of porous lava rock that constitutes the beach. Notice the views north of Lassen Peak and Eagle Peak—they'll be highlights during the return. Reach the boat ramp at 2 miles, where the trail promptly sways southwest and back into forest. Incense cedars join the pines and firs past a series of small meadows, then back to the lake's shore soon after crossing a creek at 3.4 miles.

The rest of the route is spent intimately close to the lake's edge, where you're lucky if you see some squawking geese. The views are nice of deeply forested mountains beyond pointed Lake Almanor Peninsula, as well as Dyer Mountain to the east. The 2 miles of shoreline snowshoeing feature several quiet little coves, as the route traces the numerous ins and outs of the lake's edge.

--43--

Nanny Creek

Total distance: 4.4 miles
Hiking time: 3–5 hours
Difficulty: Easy to moderate
Elevation gain: 500 feet
High point: 6,500 feet
Map: USGS Lassen Peak
Information: Lassen National Forest, Almanor Ranger District

Here's a peaceful route deep into a dark forest that features a few clearings for long-distance views to the south, gigantic rock outcrops often topped with snow, and swift Nanny Creek, a scenic spot for a picnic.

The easy course follows the forest road that bypasses McGowan Lake, steadily heading west with a handful of slight climbing bursts.

With a creek, clearings, deep forest, and open forest, wildlife abounds if you're quiet and still. Coyotes tend to trot along edges of clearings, while porcupines cling to the main trunks of conifers, high up. Deer come out late in the afternoon. The great horned owl looks like a big bundled cat, camouflaged in the evergreen boughs. Mountain chickadees flitter in the low limbs while

Route to Nanny Creek

Steller's jays squawk and rustle noisily in the branches, sometimes causing a limb to move up and down for several seconds after they lift off powerfully.

This is a good, direct route to take if heavy weather is reducing visibility, and it's especially wonderful just after a big storm, when drifts of snow are piled onto the conifer limbs. Its easy access makes it popular on weekends with cross-country skiers.

Drive to Morgan Summit at the junction of Highways 36 and 89, east of Mineral and northwest of Chester. Turn north onto Highway 89, the Lassen

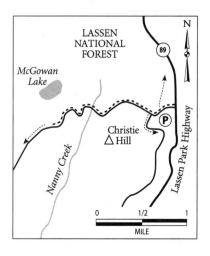

Park Highway, travel 2 miles, and then park for free in a small clearing where a snow-covered forest road (your route) leads west.

The course descends and then soon climbs in a lodgepole pine forest, which gradually becomes a dense white fir forest. Swing around a manzanita-cloaked hillside at 1.1 miles and catch views of Brokeoff Mountain to the north. Nearby Christie Hill to the south, elevation 6,559 feet, can be easily climbed here by approaching from its east flanks, then picking the easiest and safest route through white firs to the crest. You'll have to negotiate around the conifers to get views north of Lassen Peak and Brokeoff Mountain.

At 1.4 miles, a fast-flowing creek is partially blocked by large volcanic boulders. A descent ensues as incense cedars and Jeffrey pines join the now more open forest. Reach crashing Nanny Creek at 1.8 miles, and watch its froth tumble down the slope over smooth and colorful boulders. Be sure to trudge at least 0.4 mile farther, where picturesque, multi-trunked cedars mingle with a gigantic boulder outcrop. From this vista, enjoy snow-capped mountains along the northernmost range of the Sierra Nevada to the south.

--44--

Ridge Lakes and Sulphur Works

Total distance: 4.5 miles
Hiking time: 3–5 hours
Difficulty: Moderate to strenuous
Elevation gain: 1,100 feet
High point: 8,000 feet
Map: USGS Lassen Peak
Information: Lassen Volcanic National Park

When you take that last step to gain the view-filled saddle that contains the snow-covered ridge lakes, it's like discovering a Valhalla that is yours always.

Brokeoff Mountain from Lake Helen

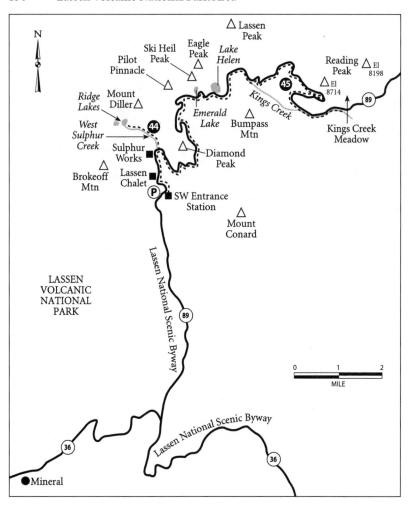

This wild and remote region requires major sweat equity—there's a 1,000-foot-in-elevation climb spanning 1.3 miles—but the route is easy to follow. Stay just on the south side of the creek that drains into Sulphur Works.

Mainly recommended for experienced and fit snowshoers, this route should be done when inclement weather doesn't threaten, and you should call ahead to determine avalanche danger. A permit is required for an overnight stay.

From Highway 36 east of Mineral, take Highway 89 (Lassen National Scenic Byway) 6 miles to the chalet and fee kiosk at the Southwest Entrance Station for Lassen Volcanic National Park. Expect to pay the park fee, although there are times when the booth is empty. Park in the first clearing beyond the chalet.

Commence a mild climb on the snow-covered park road past scattered red firs and mountain hemlocks and pleasing views of Mount Conard to the southeast. Let your nose tell you when you've reached Sulphur Works at 0.9 mile. Geothermal activity is brisk here, with bubbling puddles, mudpots, and fumaroles to look down on (stay on the fenced boardwalk) and odorous steam fumes to breathe. Sulphur Works is believed to be what's left of Mount Tehama's magma chamber steam vents.

From the north side of the parking area here, head upward, above the south banks of West Sulphur Creek. The broken forest alternates between red fir and western white pine and open spots. Look behind to gather inspiring views of the southern Cascades and the northern Sierra Nevada.

Mountain hemlocks join the forest just before reaching the Ridge Lakes nestled in a glacial cirque. In winter and spring, the two snow-covered lakes are actually joined to form one unique-shaped lake. Arguably the best views of Mount Diller to the north are found as you stroll the shoreline. This entire area was formed long ago when Mount Tehama, once a huge stratovolcano spanning 11 miles wide, collapsed.

To acquire breathtaking views from a rarely approached but doable vantage point, get to the southwest side of the lakes and head for the gap to the west. It's hard to imagine, but this slope is inundated with colorful lupines in the summer. On a clear day from the gap, you'll see the Sacramento Valley, Coast Range, Klamath Mountains, and Mount Shasta.

--45--

Lake Helen and Kings Creek Meadow

Total distance: 25 miles
Hiking time: 2–3 days
Difficulty: Moderate to strenuous
Elevation gain: 4,200 feet
High point: 8,512 feet
Maps: USGS Lassen Peak, USGS Reading Peak
Information: Lassen Volcanic National Park

Come on an amazing journey and visit two subalpine lakes, sniff the rotten-egg smell of Sulphur Works, witness countless breathtaking views, and stroll a wondrous meadow. Heavily sprinkled with throngs of tourists from Memorial

Day through Labor Day weekends, this route transforms into a wild and very remote experience when snow-clad, which is typically mid-December into early May.

Two gently curving descents lasting for several miles apiece thrill the occasional cross-country-skiing backpacker. Avalanche danger is a possibility, so call ahead for information on the latest conditions. You should plan this trip when a long stretch of clear weather is predicted. Although described as a backpack trip (permit required), feel free to abbreviate the route into a day hike of any length—you'll still get fantastic views of a volcanic wonderland along with deep peace.

From Highway 36 east of Mineral, take Highway 89 (Lassen National Scenic Byway) 6 miles to the chalet and fee kiosk at the Southwest Entrance Station for Lassen Volcanic National Park. Expect to pay the park fee, although there are times when the booth is empty. Park in the first clearing beyond the chalet.

Begin a mild climb on the snow-covered park road, which you stay on the whole way. You'll pass scattered red firs and mountain hemlocks and pleasing views of Mount Conard to the southeast. Let your nose tell you when you've reached Sulphur Works at 0.9 mile. Geothermal activity is brisk here, with bubbling puddles to look down on (stay on the fenced path along this brief side trip) and odorous steam fumes to breathe.

Continue a moderate ascent until you face huge volcanic spires atop imposing Diamond Peak that appear as though they'll topple and crash loudly. After another mile of climbing, appreciate outrageous views of Lassen Peak, Eagle Peak, and Ski Heil Peak nearby. The route keeps snaking higher, rendering improved views of dome-shaped Pilot Pinnacle beginning at 4.8 miles.

One mile farther, reach Emerald Lake, where a superb view of Brokeoff Mountain awaits just above the northeast shore. This mountain is a remnant of ancient Mount Tehama, which once soared to an elevation of about 11,500 feet, with a 5-mile diameter. Only 0.4 mile farther, an incomparable view of Lassen Peak is attained from above the south shore of oval-shaped Lake Helen at 8,400 feet in elevation. The enticing shoreline of this large lake deserves to be explored, with the intense south face of Lassen Peak staring down all the while. It last erupted in 1917, dramatically altering the topography.

Climb 0.3 mile to tremendous views down on Lake Helen, topped by snow-capped Brokeoff Mountain, Mount Diller, and Ski Heil Peak. You soon begin a long and winding descent as the scattered, stunted specimens of whitebark pines (five needles to a bunch) rapidly disappear, giving way to an even mix of red firs and mountain hemlocks again.

Kings Creek and Lassen Peak

After about 5 miles of exhilarating downhill, featuring countless views to the southeast of expansive Juniper Lake, your route climaxes into large Kings Creek Meadow. You've come this far, be sure to traipse to the southeast boundary of the meadow for one of the most photographed views of Lassen Peak, featuring icy clear and swirling Kings Creek in the foreground.

--46--

Cinder Cone and Fantastic Lava Beds

Total distance: 5 miles or longer
Hiking time: 4–7 hours
Difficulty: Moderate
Elevation gain: 800 feet
High point: 6,900 feet
Maps: USGS Prospect Peak, USGS Mount Harkness
Information: Lassen Volcanic National Park

The large lakes, acres of rock piles, and snowy miniature hills that surround Cinder Cone make for a fairy tale setting so surreal that it's like visiting an alien world. You get to snowshoe by it and then look down on it all atop perfectly symmetrical Cinder Cone, the centerpiece of this classic, volcanic wonderland.

This trek can easily be extended into an awesome 14-mile-long backpack loop (get permit) by snowshoeing through the lodgepole pine, Jeffrey pine, and fir forest to shallow Snag Lake, then around the aspen-dotted eastern shore of Butte Lake. You may have to park on the side of the road from 1 to several

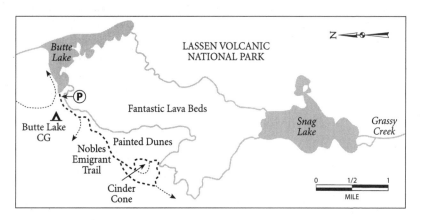

Painted Dunes below Cinder Cone

miles short of the trailhead. Call ahead for the snow conditions. Cross-country skiers sometimes claim Cinder Cone's broad summit, then get thrilled by zipping steeply down the snowy slopes. Call ahead to obtain avalanche danger.

From the junction of Highways 89 and 44, take 44 south for 12 miles, then turn west on a gravel and cinder road signed for Butte Lake. If lack of snow permits, continue to its end 6.7 miles farther, then park near Butte Lake's north shore.

If snow forces you to start from the side of the road, you'll be trudging up mostly level, open forest, past western junipers, Jeffrey pines, and tobacco brush on the snow-covered access road. Otherwise, follow along the snow-covered, historic Nobles Emigrant Trail, used in the mid-1800s by thousands of pioneers. Unless there's been a recent snow, pre-laid tracks should make this route easy to follow. Wander in an open conifer forest bordered by the tremendous piles of gray-black basalt that form Fantastic Lava Beds. Glassy fragments of quartz crystals helped form these boulder hills as lava cooled from several eruptions of Cinder Cone.

The ancient Jeffrey and ponderosa pines tower over the adjacent, flat forest floor here, with initial views of Lassen Peak and neighboring Crescent Crater appearing at 0.4 mile. Look for the huge and photogenic white stump snag on the trail's right side (kids like to climb it) just before reaching the trail fork at Cinder Cone's base at 0.8 mile.

The steep climb up Cinder Cone, gaining 700 feet in elevation from its base, is made even more challenging since each footstep sinks and slips into porous cinders. Establish a patient trudge, and pause often to admire tree-covered Prospect Peak to the north and Lassen Peak to the west.

By circumnavigating Cinder Cone, there are breathtaking photos of the previously mentioned views as well as contrasting Butte and Snag Lakes separated by Fantastic Lava Beds and the hydrothermally altered orange and gray ash piles called Painted Dunes. Gaze down on or descend into the huge and cavernous reverse cone in the center of Cinder Cone. The bottom of the charcoal-colored pit is dappled with pumice and larger basalt rocks.

Just beyond the northwest outer edge of Cinder Cone's high rim, a handful of semi-wind-protected mountain mahogany shrubs poke through the snow. A scattering of dwarfed lodgepole pines and a handful of even smaller Jeffrey pines stand out in an otherwise stark landscape of smooth and symmetrical slopes.

Descend the southern slope of Cinder Cone and loop around the cone's base in a delightfully alien setting. Here the snowy swirls of Painted Dunes mingle with the moonlike boulders of Fantastic Lava Beds. The props for a sci-fi movie are in place here—odd-looking big rocks strewn about with an occasional child-sized conifer punctuating the whiteness.

--47--

Baker Lake and Hat Creek Rim

Total distance: Up to 7 miles
Hiking time: 1–5 hours
Difficulty: Easy to moderate
Elevation gain: 500 feet
High point: 5,300 feet
Map: USGS topo Old Station
Information: Hat Creek Ranger District–Lassen National Forest

Much of the volcanic landscape just northeast of Lassen Park is flat, adorned with youthful forests where many plots of conifers began life together, are

West Prospect Peak along Baker Lake route

stunted in cinder, or both. The terrain is gentle, with hints of high desert and progressively sloped volcanoes.

This is the tone of this remote route, which takes you into a large, tree-dotted meadow, the edge of Hat Creek Rim at its steepest section, and finally to shallow and probably snow-coated Baker Lake. This is a superb excursion following a cold front that dropped snow at this low of an elevation. Call ahead, or get set to try another route nearby at a higher elevation if there is no or too little snow here.

Chances are you'll have the entire route to yourself, even on holidays. Perhaps old tracks from cross-country skis, snowshoes, and/or dogs can be spotted. Speaking of tracks, watch for fresh footprints of predators, such as coyote and long-tailed weasel, or leaf eaters, such as mule deer or snow rabbit.

Park for free in the turnout near the Forest Road 33N20 sign off Highway 44. It's a few miles above the junction of Highways 89 and 44 northeast of Old Station, and 2.2 miles southeast of the Hat Creek Rim Overlook sign.

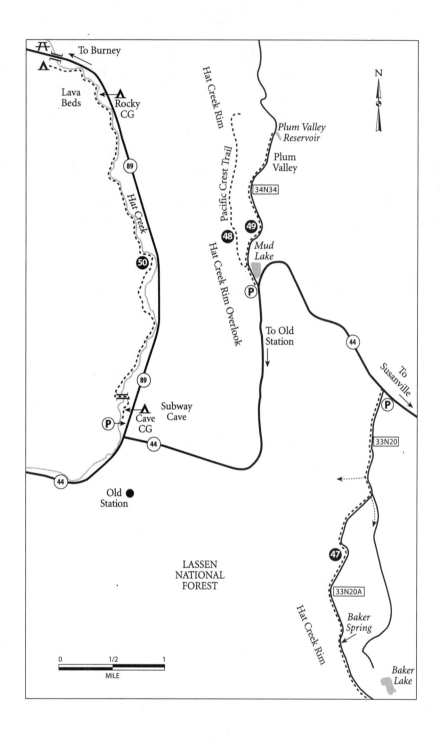

Gradually climb east on cinder road 33N20, ignoring branching roads until you get to the most obvious junction at 1.2 miles, where you climb right onto signed Forest Road 33N20A. Stay on this mostly flat route all the way to Baker Lake. The scenery continues to consist of strewn volcanic boulders and young adult Jeffrey pines, most of them the same size, accentuated by antelope brush, spindly limbed rabbit brush, and occasional greenleaf manzanita.

After commencing a slight downhill at 1.6 miles, look for straight-on views of heavily tree-clad West Prospect Peak looming to the south. The trees gradually diminish on the east side, and it looks more and more like a large, snow-covered meadow you're bordering.

When you can clearly see the edge of Hat Creek Rim at 3 miles some 75 yards to the west, scamper over for a breathtaking view of Lassen Peak, West Prospect Peak, and Potato Butte up close. Farther on and to the north by northwest, adore the brushy and rocky Hat Creek Valley, capped by Sugarloaf Mountain, the Thousand Lakes Mountains, and Burney Mountain. Mount Shasta glistens to the north. You'll be no doubt driven to move to various vantage points to get varying views past the western junipers, mountain mahoganies, and ponderosa pines.

Picnic on the rim's edge or wait to eat among the occasional lodgepole pines at Baker Lake at 3.5 miles.

--48--

Hat Creek Rim and Pacific Crest Trail

Total distance: 5 miles
Hiking time: 3–5 hours
Difficulty: Easy to moderate
Elevation gain: 200 feet
High point: 4,900 feet
Map: USGS Old Station
Information: Hat Creek Ranger District–Lassen National Forest

Arguably, the Hat Creek Rim punctuates the Lassen National Forest landscape more uniquely and more noticeably than anything else. Rising abruptly some 700 feet above the Hat Creek Valley, the Hat Creek Rim makes a nearly straight line across the countryside for more than 10 miles. ˋ

From the valley floor, the rim looks greenish gray. That color is fully

Burney Mountain from Hat Creek Rim Overlook

understood when you're on the rim, picking and choosing your way around lava boulders, stunted conifers, and desert chaparral.

Wander along an interesting stretch of the Pacific Crest Trail in a high-desert transition zone, where open forest interacts with dry, flat highlands blanketed with tiny-leafed, tough shrubs. The first highlight is the newly constructed Hat Creek Rim Overlook, which offers an ideal, clear, and photogenic view across the Hat Creek Valley.

Call ahead to make sure there's enough snow, and be prepared to do another nearby route described in this book instead that's higher in elevation. Be warned—even with enough snow you'll have to carefully negotiate snowshoes over twiggy ground covers and bumpy rocks.

From the junction of Highways 89 and 44 just northeast of Old Station, drive 2.8 miles up Highway 44 to the sign indicating Hat Creek Rim Overlook, then park for free on the side of the small clearing.

Begin heading due west on the snow-covered paved road, crossing the gate and noting that the road you pass on the right makes for a delightful return route (Route 49). The way climbs gently in an open forest of tall and lean incense cedars and ponderosa pines.

After 0.5 mile, reach the impressively built Hat Creek Rim Overlook, a deck that extends over the lip of the rim to reveal a top-of-the-world view over the Hat Creek Valley. To the southwest, Lassen Peak (a plug-dome volcano) and neighboring Chaos Crags dominate. Straight ahead to the west, cone-shaped and mostly forested Sugarloaf Mountain, a young cinder cone volcano, looms. North of it, there's Freaner Peak followed by Burney Mountain and Mount Shasta farther in the distance. The overlook is equipped with picnic tables, restrooms, and interpretive signs. It's quickly become a busy place in the non-snow months, but you're apt to have the place to yourself, enjoying arguably better views here in winter and spring than summer and fall.

Signed Pacific Crest Trail takes off from the northwest end of the parking lot. Following it will be a challenge. If you lose it, pick and choose your way near the rim's edge for several miles if desired. Along the way, you'll encounter an impressive array of native trees and shrubs, including mountain mahogany, antelope brush, rabbit brush, western juniper, incense cedar, ponderosa pine, and sugar pine. Our route stops at 2.5 miles, just as it begins a steady descent. At this juncture, you can cut east to pick up the Plum Valley route, which goes south to your car.

--49--

Plum Valley

Total distance: 4.5 miles or longer
Hiking time: 1–3 hours
Difficulty: Easy
Elevation gain: 250 feet
High point: 4,900 feet
Map: USGS Old Station
Information: Hat Creek Ranger District–Lassen National Forest

What a difference some snow makes. It transforms this otherwise ordinary volcanic landscape into a tranquil yet wild scene.

The tall conifers here take center stage, especially when their boughs droop with fresh snow. It's roughly an equal mix of incense cedars and ponderosa pines with an occasional western juniper interspersed. If snow falls during this journey, you can stand beneath the biggest cedar available and stay mostly snowflake-free while watching the silent show.

Petite Plum Valley is more like a shelf bottom, where a densely forested cliff borders its eastern edge and a remote region of the Hat Creek Rim adorns the western flanks. Long ago, four Native American groups—Yahi, Maidu, Yana, and Atsugewi—would choose a route like this for hunting, fleeing for warmer and lower ground as the first snows arrived.

From the junction of Highways 89 and 44 just northeast of Old Station, drive 2.8 miles up Highway 44 to the sign indicating Hat Creek Rim Overlook, then park for free on the side of the small clearing (see map on page 158).

Brisk with vehicles on their way to Plum Valley Reservoir in late spring through autumn, Forest Road 34N34 (your route) becomes a wide pathway where snowshoers can walk and talk calmly side by side the whole way to this tiny I-shaped body of water (unrecognizable when snow-covered).

This is an ideal excursion following a cold front that dropped snow at this low of an elevation. Call ahead, or get set to try another route nearby at a higher elevation if there is no or too little snow here.

You may have the entire route to yourself, even on holidays. Perhaps old tracks from cross-country skis, snowshoes, and/or dogs can be spotted.

Commence a brief and gentle climb with the sun (if it's shining) on your back appearing through the dappled shade of high-limbed native conifers. Brace yourself on clear and windy days for frigid north winds in your face.

Note the clearing on the right at 0.3 mile where small and shallow Mud Lake is buried in snow, then detect the welcomed silence as you leave curving

Ponderosa pine

Highway 44 way behind. Daydreams and deep thoughts will likely absorb you as each easily laid snowshoe print gradually enters Plum Valley. The trip can readily be extended beyond 2-mile-long Plum Valley. Another 3 miles brings you to Grassy Lake (after a brief climb leads to a big flat).

--*50*--
Hat Creek

Total distance: Up to 8 miles
Hiking time: 4–6 hours
Difficulty: Easy to moderate
Elevation gain: 400 feet
High point: 4,300 feet
Map: USGS Old Station
Information: Hat Creek Ranger District–Lassen National Forest

Follow the raging course of icy Hat Creek roughly from its halfway point to its climax into the Pit River. Hat Creek's amazing journey begins as snowmelt high on the north-facing flank of Lassen Peak. Its crystal clear waters embellish Paradise Meadows, widen into a marsh that was once Hat Lake, and finally evolve into the powerful force that this route covers. The copious cascades and mini-waterfalls become a robust burst from midwinter through spring over this part of the creek. It's a constant, loud crash that stirs the senses—toss a stick in and watch it vanish instantly in the surge.

Your route traces the creek's edge the whole way, but often doesn't have enough snow for snowshoeing. Call ahead for snow conditions. Be ready to do another nearby route described in this book that's higher in elevation. Even with enough snow, there are parts of the route where you'll have to carefully negotiate snowshoes over bumpy rocks and twiggy ground covers.

From the junction of Highways 44 and 89, turn north onto Highway 89 and drive 0.3 mile. Turn left into Cave Campground, go 30 yards, and then park for free in the small lot on the left (see map on page 158). Cross the wooden bridge at Hat Creek and pick up the trail on the right.

Reach a concrete bridge and a gorge of rapidly rushing water at 0.5 mile where a cluster of tall ponderosa pines thrives. Hemmed into a narrow slot by solid lava rock, this series of cascades and mini-waterfalls is an intense symphony composed by nature.

Western junipers along Hat Creek

Observe a gorgeous grove of white-trunked aspen trees at 1 mile. It's peculiar to see so many towering ponderosa pines and incense cedars, two species that basically detest wet feet, interspersed with aspens and other riparian trees such as alders and willows. Just a few yards beyond the banks, admire a labyrinth of chaparral shrubs such as greenleaf manzanita, antelope bitterbrush, mountain mahogany, and rabbit goldenweed dotted with western junipers and California sage. The twisted trunks of the bigger bushes create a tangled and cluttered picture.

Bushes outnumber the trees and partially cover the continuous views. Forested and cone-shaped Sugarloaf Peak to the west is the most prominent mountain at first. The glimpses of Lassen Peak and Chaos Crags are more obvious on the return trip. The west-facing visage of the steep Hat Creek Rim is a constant companion. Views of Freaner Peak and Burney Mountain farther northwest become more frequent after reaching a second but smaller aspen grove at 1.8 miles, followed by a rock-encased cascade 0.2 mile farther.

After passing another small waterfall at 2.2 miles, the trail briefly enters a forest strip consisting of the previously mentioned conifers as well as the occasional white fir and sugar pine with a snowberry-dominated ground cover. A steady cascade splashes over narrow and rocky banks for 0.25 mile, decreasing only after culminating in another mini-waterfall at 2.7 miles.

At 3.1 miles, the first sighting of Magee and Crater Peaks to the west are featured from a vantage point near some aspens and a huge, multiple-trunked alder tree. Enter another forest strip, which promptly leads to a wooden bridge at 3.8 miles and Rocky Campground.

Adding visual variety, the trail then dissects some basalt talus, then rises gently so you can look down into the canyon to admire Hat Creek to Bridge Camp.

--*51*--
West Prospect Peak

Total distance: Up to 24 miles
Hiking time: 2–3 days
Difficulty: Strenuous
Elevation gain: 3,600 feet
High point: 8,174 feet
Map: USGS West Prospect Peak
Information: Hat Creek Ranger District-Lassen National Forest

In terms of girth, West Prospect Peak rates among the mightiest in Lassen National Forest. And no wonder there's a lookout atop this lofty, densely conifered mountain—the panorama reveals a plethora of place names and well-known volcanoes.

Bowl-shaped West Prospect Peak itself is a shield dome volcano, and so is its nearest neighbor, Prospect Peak. That explains why they look like twins.

To enlist for this epic endeavor, the body should be fit and the soul may no doubt be crazed, for those are the ideal traits to accomplish this mission. Actually, the journey might be shorter if lack of low-elevation snow allows you to drive a few miles along this route.

Rest assured, you'll most likely have the whole place to yourself for days as you travel past scenic Hat Creek, along the low flanks of Badger Mountain, and then up the south face of view-laden West Prospect Peak.

Drive a few miles southwest from Old Station or a few miles northeast from the North Entrance of Lassen Volcanic National Park on Highway 44. Park for

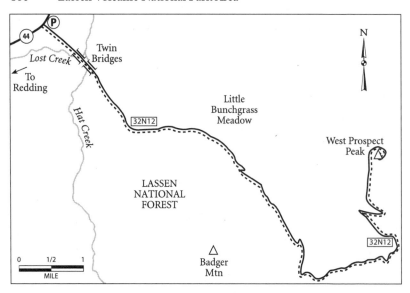

free in the small turnout on the southeast side of the road, near the metal sign for West Prospect Peak and Twin Bridges. If Forest Road 32N12 is clear of snow, continue to the snow line (it's best to call ahead) and then pull over to the side of the road.

Traipse in a level and open ponderosa pine forest for 1 mile, then cross icy clear Lost Creek. A minute or so later, cross photogenic Hat Creek on a bridge identical to Lost Creek's (Twin Bridges).

Over the next 2 miles, several roads lead elsewhere—stay on course as you admire head-on views of looming Badger Mountain and West Prospect Peak. The snow just off trail may show uneven dips because of the profuse ground cover of pinemat manzanita.

At 3.2 miles, the route reaches the foot of Badger Mountain and begins steady but moderate climbing. Incense cedars and white firs join the pines in continued mostly open forest.

At 6.8 miles, cross a creek and leave Badger Mountain behind, climbing steadily east in a mixed forest mainly of white fir, lodgepole pine, and Jeffrey pine. One and a half miles farther, the climbing intensifies as you veer south and begin the official ascent of West Prospect Peak. After 1 mile of climbing, Forest Road 32N12 zigzags and eventually shows off several big piles of lava rocks below to the west. The climb now alternates between sunny and shady spots in a red fir, western white pine, mountain hemlock, and Jeffrey pine forest where the great horned owl looks like a big cat hidden in the boughs.

Note that the conifers become more dwarfed over the final mile, allowing more sunlight for high-mountain chaparral shrubs to thrive, such as currant, alpine spiraea, manzanita, and bush chinquapin. Look for Clark's nutcrackers frolicking in the twigs.

From various vantage points atop West Prospect Peak at 12 miles, an ideal panorama unfolds. To the west, Raker Peak moves your gaze to Lassen Peak and Chaos Crags. Swinging south, Mount Harkness fronts the Sierra Nevada in the hazy distance. The Warner Mountains anchor the northeastern horizon beyond a series of mountains that get progressively drier in the desert regions of Northern California. Arguably the best views lie to the north, where Sugarloaf Mountain, Freaner Peak, and Burney Mountain guard the sprawling Hat Creek Valley.

Jeffrey pines towards West Prospect Peak

--*52*--

Reflection Lake and Manzanita Lake

Total distance: 4 miles
Hiking time: 3–4 hours
Difficulty: Easy
Elevation gain: 200 feet
High point: 5,900 feet
Map: USGS Manzanita Lake
Information: Lassen Volcanic National Park

It seems only fair that paradise, especially in wintertime, should be earned. Such is not the case with these two precious jewels for lakes. Reflection and Manzanita Lakes are so approachable, so easy to explore, it seems there should be some sweat equity to endure. There isn't.

From the shapely shorelines and golden willow shoots to the incomparable views of Chaos Crags and Lassen Peak, the scenes on this snowshoe trek can be appreciated as if you were at a favorite art museum. For this is the time

Chaos Crags from Manzanita Lake

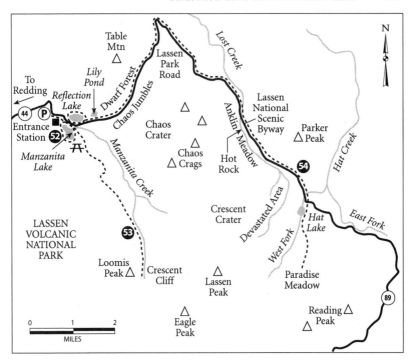

when these contrasting lakes are nicely iced over with a crown of snow, and the countless bright blue Steller's jays squawk and thrash loudly amid the conifers, interrupting what would be otherwise total peace.

Although this photogenic region is brisk with tourists in the summer, you're apt to share it with perhaps an occasional snowshoer or cross-country skier during the winter months.

From Redding, take Highway 44 east for 48 scenic miles and turn right into signed Lassen Volcanic National Park. You may have to park on the side of the park road there, or in the large paved lot several yards farther. A fee may be charged, especially on weekends.

Head up the park road until you reach the southern shore of Reflection Lake, then try to follow the 0.7-mile interpretive loop that reaches Lily Pond, which may be an interesting mission if tracks aren't already laid. This unique side trip wanders quietly in a mixed forest featuring nine different kinds of native conifers: incense cedar, red fir, white fir, Jeffrey pine, ponderosa pine, sugar pine, Douglas fir, mountain hemlock, and lodgepole pine.

After finishing the Lily Pond side excursion, retrace your tracks to the eastern shore of Reflection Lake, then head north, tracing the lake's edge. When you get to the northeastern shore at 1.1 miles, look back for an enticing view of Chaos Crags and Lassen Peak.

Access Manzanita Lake by following Reflection Lake's shoreline midway along its western edge, cross the park road, and then head left (south) to trace the curving shoreline. Note the numerous pine logs scattered across the snowscape—it will take five decades or so for them to rot into a ground cover of wood chips. Veer away from the lake temporarily to get around a thick grove of willows. Manzanita Creek widens before easing into the lake at 2 miles. Note the giant ponderosa pine next to a pair of tables and an equally tall conifer snag.

Pass the boat launch site and hug the shoreline for the final mile, noting the tiny islands of willows scattered along the way. You'll frequently duck under stalwart white fir and Jeffrey pine—they'll serve to frame your views across the lake. Watch for a handful of black cottonwoods at 3.3 miles, their ash-white trunks accentuate the western shoreline. Impenetrable thickets of manzanita, hence the lake's namesake, thrive a few yards from the western shore. Just past the cottonwoods, views of Eagle Peak and Lassen Peak show up, and they keep getting better around each bend.

Photos are virtually guaranteed to be great of Lassen Peak, Eagle Peak, Chaos Crags, and eventually Loomis Peak off to the west, all with the serene and snowy lake in the foreground. If you're here in the late afternoon, you'll catch dramatic shadows cast across the lake and sensational highlights on the mountains during sunny days. Cross the lake's outlet stream and look for icicles. Capture a final view at the rustic stone A-frame close to the park road.

--53--

Manzanita Creek

Total distance: 8 miles
Hiking time: 6–10 hours
Difficulty: Moderate
Elevation gain: 1,100 feet
High point: 6,900 feet
Maps: USGS Lassen Peak, USGS Manzanita Lake
Information: Lassen Volcanic National Park

Every creek has a beginning, and this route traces Manzanita Creek upward to its high-mountain source—a scenic meadow. Along the way you'll get awesome views of breathtakingly imposing Chaos Crags, a volcano formed

Manzanita Lake, willows, and Lassen Peak

over a millennium ago when viscous lava welled up for more than 500 yards. Part of the way lingers lovingly close to chilly and crystal clear Manzanita Creek, and you'll also wander in high meadows while checking out mountain views.

Chances are you'll be trekking alongside previously laid cross country-ski tracks, enjoying immense solitude in a remote forest where pine martens are elusive, black bears hibernate, and the great horned owl resembles a big cat in the conifer boughs.

From Redding, take Highway 44 east for 48 scenic miles and turn right into signed Lassen Volcanic National Park. You may have to park on the side of the park road there, or in the large paved lot several yards farther (see map on page 169). A fee may be charged, especially on weekends.

Snowshoe up the park road, pausing often to admire shapely Manzanita Lake, with bright yellow/orange willow branches adorning parts of its shore. At 0.6 mile, bear right at a road junction, cross Manzanita Creek Bridge, and wander past Manzanita Lake Campground as views to the southeast of Chaos Crags inspire.

You'll probably be enticed to roam in the open field on the left for better views of twin-peaked Chaos Crags, which is best photographed in the late afternoon. This large, flat field features a bizarre mosaic of juvenile Jeffrey pines and a mix of thriving and ghostly-limbed, dead greenleaf manzanita.

It's a good idea to set a slow but steady pace as you ascend continually in an open Jeffrey pine, white fir, and red fir forest. Backdoor views of Eagle Peak, Lassen Peak, and Chaos Crags kick in along a flat stretch of trail at 1.8 miles. These partially shielded scenes soon disappear temporarily, but revel in the whisperlike silence as you progress past occasional bush chinquapin with its shiny yellow leaf undersides. The previously mentioned peaks reappear when you reach a small meadow at 2.2 miles. Western white pines begin showing up as you approach nature's ideal mix of sudsy rapids and icy clear water at a bridge crossing at 2.5 miles. The invigorating crashing thunder of swift and narrow Manzanita Creek sets a rhythm for the rest of the route. Steep and ominous Loomis Peak appears to the southwest next to an expansive alder thicket at 3 miles. The way now stays mostly flat past snowy clearings bordered by lichen-covered red firs.

At journey's end, Manzanita Creek can be heard from a meadow blasting down a steep slope near the doorstep of Loomis Peak. Explore arguably the best strip of the creek from the large clearing, featuring mini-waterfalls, curving cascades, and bubbly whirlpools.

On the return trip, note the stark contrast in form and texture between the Thousand Lakes mountain cluster far to the north and nearby Loomis Peak.

--*54*--

Paradise Meadow

Total distance: 23 miles
Hiking time: 2–3 days
Difficulty: Moderate
Elevation gain: 1,400 feet
High point: 7,000 feet
Maps: USGS Manzanita Lake, USGS Reading Peak, USGS Prospect Peak
Information: Lassen Volcanic National Park

Roam over a land so eerily strange that you wouldn't be totally shocked if some pterodactyls flew by. That's because there are so many dwarfed conifers, rolling hillocks of jumbled rocks, and a devastated area caused by Lassen Peak's volcanic eruption in 1917.

What a difference the snow makes. It softens the prehistoric-looking landscape, and since scarcely a soul is around, things are quiet, inviting reflection. An occasional cross-country skier might share the snow-covered park road with you until you break away from the road for the final 1.5 miles along Hat Creek to Paradise Meadow. Along the way, you'll get great views of snow-clad Lassen Peak and mostly snow-free Chaos Crags, with its steep and rocky flanks that shed the white stuff. Crescent Crater and Reading Peak seem more noticeable in the winter with their shiny blankets of snow. Spacious Paradise Meadow, backed by the precipitous cliff of Reading Peak's north face, makes you feel special—like you're way in the middle of nowhere.

It's best to do this route when a long stretch of agreeable weather is predicted. Although described as a backpack trip (permit required), feel free to abbreviate the trip into any desired duration, and you'll still find seclusion and photogenic views.

From Redding, take Highway 44 east for 48 scenic miles and turn right into signed Lassen Volcanic National Park. You may have to park on the side of the park road there, or in the large paved lot several yards farther (see map on page 169). A fee may be charged, especially on weekends.

Snowshoe up the park road, halting often to cherish shapely Manzanita Lake, decorated with bright yellow/orange willow branches along parts of its shore. After about 1 mile, the park road veers northeast, leaving the lake in an open forest of ponderosa pine, Jeffrey pine, Douglas fir, and white fir. The imposing north face of orange/rust-colored Chaos Crags blocks Lassen Peak

Steller's Jay

for an extended stretch. You're soon in the midst of Chaos Jumbles, a series of dinky dips and hills sporting occasional stunted Jeffrey pines. These miniature and undernourished pines feature a yellowish cast on their needles. This is because the soil they're growing in is lean and undeveloped. This science-fiction-like scene continues for about 1 mile, stretching northward to the base of wide, thickly conifered Table Mountain and southeastward to the base of Chaos Crags.

At 3.8 miles, the route bends sharply southeast and is uneventful and relaxing for another 2.5 miles as it climbs gently in a peaceful forest of Jeffrey pine and white fir. A narrow and flat strip of quaking aspens on the west side of the park road called Anklin Meadow is reached at 7.8 miles, along with a huge brown boulder called Hot Rock. A bit over 1 mile farther, notice that Devastated Area is an almost mile-wide strip of talus and strewn boulders that killed virtually everything in its downward path during the 1917 volcanic eruption of Lassen Peak. The forest is gradually returning, but because the conifers are still juvenile, there are great views of Crescent Crater and Lassen Peak here.

Reach signed Hat Creek at 10.2 miles and leave the park road while tracing the east bank of the icy clear creek. Right off, pass what is left of Hat Lake. A huge mudflow swept down from Mount Lassen in 1915 and dammed the West Fork of Hat Creek, creating smallish Hat Lake. The lake then filled with stream sediments, leaving a tiny pond, which is gradually turning into the meadow that surrounds it.

After a final glimpse of Lassen Peak, climb in a mixed forest of red fir, western white pine, and mountain hemlock. At 1.3 miles from Hat Lake, reach an inspirational, multi-terraced, 20-foot cascade, then press on 200 yards to Paradise Meadow. West Fork of Hat Creek slows to a lazy cruise here, splitting through the expansive meadow, featuring an attention-getting view of Reading Peak to the south.

--*55*--

Crystal and Baum Lakes

Total distance: Up to 5 miles
Hiking time: 2–3 hours
Difficulty: Easy
Elevation gain: 100 feet
High point: 3,000 feet
Map: USGS Cassel
Information: PG&E

Especially on a clear winter's day, the tranquil waters of Crystal and Baum Lakes dramatically reflect the snowy visages of Burney Mountain to the west and Mount Shasta to the north. It's a placid place where osprey, hawks, and migratory ducks and geese soar aloft. Take a twilight trek and hope to experience an award-winning sunset, quite common after a cold-front snowstorm leaves behind a blanket of cumulus and cirrus clouds on the horizon.

The easy-to-follow route traces the lakes' shorelines, showing off hatchery-released rainbow and brook trout. A good snow often lingers for days, getting crustier as it slowly melts in this typically cold basin. But snow at this low elevation is occasional, so call ahead to determine if there is enough for snowshoeing. Even as snow is falling, it's hard to get lost. Besides the waterbirds mentioned above, yellow pine forest birds flitter in the meadow strips and the lower limbs of the many trees. Look for woodpeckers, purple finches, and warblers.

From the intersection of Highways 89 and 299 East, drive 299 East for 2 miles, then turn south onto paved Cassel Road. Go 2 more miles, turn left at the sign for Crystal Lake Fish Hatchery, drive another mile, and then turn left into the paved parking lot and park for free.

Traipse over to the dam that separates the two lakes, then head west from the north side and skirt the shore of scenic and photogenic Crystal Lake. For the first mile or so, western juniper, sagebrush, squawbush, and ceanothus accompany you, along with Oregon white oak and black oak, which display attractive shades of orange and rust often into early winter.

The next mile (the south side) passes through an open ponderosa pine forest where clear views of Mount Shasta are frequent. Look for white pelicans patrolling the gray waters of Crystal Lake.

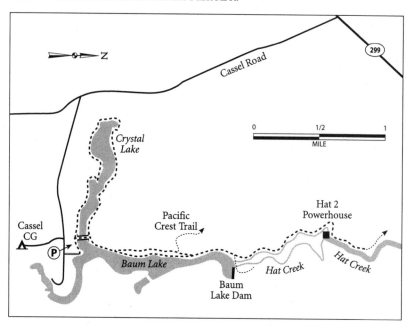

The 1.5-mile way along Baum Lake's west shore (including a portion of the Pacific Crest Trail) also commences at the north side of the dam. Follow the obvious narrow trail north, and note ponderosa pines growing close to the water's edge while deciduous oaks dominate the slopes on the left.

The way soon splits. The upper route travels mid-slope, crosses a fence, and then reaches another fork. The Pacific Crest Trail heads left and uphill, but you stay right and soon reach the lower trail, which always runs along the lakeshore. Continue past lava rock talus, negotiate a brush area along a small creek, and then reach Baum Lake Dam. For more snowshoeing, take a trail from the east side of the dam some 400 yards down to Hat Creek's banks, or snowshoe north along the canal that soon reaches Hat 2 Powerhouse.

Castle Lake

MOUNT SHASTA AREA

Around Interstate 5

--*56*--

Castle Creek and Horse Heaven Meadow

Total distance: 2–14 miles
Hiking time: 2–7 hours or overnight
Difficulty: Moderate
Elevation gain: 1,400 feet
High point: 4,200 feet
Map: USGS Dunsmuir
Information: Mount Shasta Ranger District, Shasta-Trinity National Forest

It doesn't happen often, but when bustling Castle Creek's boulders become billowy snow pillows, a snowshoer is in for a special treat. Here's a wild yet peaceful route far from the hurried crowds, with a good chance you can have it all to yourself. Long gone are the chugging logging trucks that roar around

Boulder Peak from Castle Creek

the numerous bends of Castle Creek Road, your route when it's snow covered. Call ahead for snow conditions. This little-known snowshoe and cross-country ski journey is loaded with refreshing creekside scenery and wonderful views of snowy Flume Creek Ridge and Grey Rocks.

Watch closely for photo opportunities, including Castle Creek with the snow white and steep granite of Grey Rocks as an ideal backdrop. By occasionally glancing behind you or waiting for the return trip, there are plenty of views of Castle Crags from this rare vantage point to the west.

Because this route includes several creeks and seasonal streams full of moving water, combined with a mix of chaparral, meadow, and dense forest, winter wildlife viewing is at a premium on this varied course. Deep blue Steller's jays squawk in the pines while mountain chickadees flitter in the brush. Woodpeckers may be drilling into tree trunks while red-tailed hawks circle above clearings looking for pocket gophers, chipmunks, and gray squirrels. Wily coyotes are best observed from above, where they may be trotting along the banks of Castle Creek. Listen for the sound of branches snapping in the shrubbery, for it may be deer. Harmless bobcats like to watch you from a few yards away, hidden behind a big boulder or camouflaged in brush.

Because the snow-covered road is so easy to follow, this trip can be done even while it's snowing. There are a lot of incense cedars to stand beneath for protection. The key to enjoying this endeavor as a snowshoe route is to go during or after snow graces this low-elevation region. (Call ahead to check on snow conditions.) If snow is still too skimpy, opt for snowshoe routes in the nearby Castle Lake and Heart Lake area (Routes 59 and 60). If you spend the night, obtain a wilderness permit. If energy and/or time forbid, consider shortening this route to any desired length.

Reach the I-5 Castle Crags/Castella Exit 6 miles south of Dunsmuir and 48 miles north of Redding. Go west on Castle Creek Road and pass signed Castle Crags State Park within 1 mile. Drive to the snow line where the road is unplowed and find a spot to park for free on the side of the road.

The first mile or so is mostly level, showing off lovely scenes involving wide and bouldery Castle Creek as the main attraction. Incense cedars, Douglas firs, and ponderosa pines frame intermittent views of Grey Rocks, a granitic mountain that stands guard solo over the Castle Creek basin from the west. The narrow, snow-covered road snakes upward and crosses alder-lined Castle Creek at about 2 miles. More and more ceanothus and manzanita scrub join the open sections of the forest along with canyon live oaks. The climb abates for a while as views southward of Flume Creek Ridge take center stage.

Brief and moderate descents alternate with mostly level trudging over the

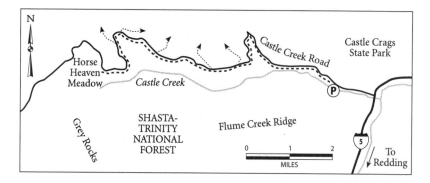

next couple of miles, where a few alternate roads branch from the main road. Always take the more obvious Castle Creek Road, which usually heads west. At 1.5 miles before reaching Horse Heaven Meadow, the course veers southward and reveals more close-up views of Grey Rocks, now to the south. At 6.5 miles, the road angles west for the final 0.5 mile of easy snowshoeing to pleasant and isolated Horse Heaven Meadow.

--*57*--

McCloud River Waterfalls

Total distance: 3.2 miles
Hiking time: 3–4 hours
Difficulty: Easy
Elevation gain: 200 feet
High point: 3,600 feet
Map: USGS Lake McCloud
Information: McCloud Ranger District, Shasta-Trinity National Forest

This trio of robust waterfalls, when surrounded by a blanket of snow, seems extra special and photogenic. Tune into a wild river that teases you with the first waterfall, entices you with the second, and then blows the doors down with the third waterfall. Skipping Upper McCloud Falls would be like walking out of a mystery movie two-thirds of the way through.

All three of these misting falls are encompassed in granite, but the similarities end there. In contrast, Lower Falls are tame while Middle Falls exude a spiritual feel where a soul can hark back to the days when the Wintu Indians must have found deep peace on one of the huge rocks at the scene. Intense

Lower McCloud Falls

Upper Falls aren't as photogenic as Middle Falls but are arguably the most breathtaking and certainly carry the most water force.

This trip has a lot to admire for little energy expense. Note that you can make the journey much longer (even a backpack trip) by continuing on a new trail section that traces the banks of fast-flowing McCloud River. After 14 miles,

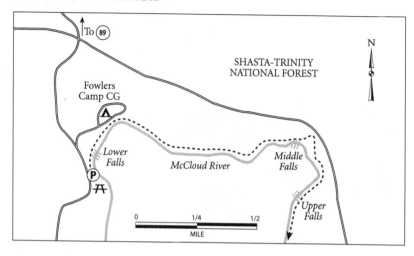

you exit a remote river region into the tiny community of Algoma. The key to this snowshoe endeavor is to seize the chance to do it during the handful of periods when snow lingers at this lower elevation. Call ahead to check on snow conditions.

From I-5 south of Mount Shasta, take Highway 89 east 15 miles (5 miles past McCloud). Turn right onto the paved road signed for river access and Fowlers Camp Campground. Go 0.6 mile, continue straight at a road branch, head right 50 yards farther, continue 0.6 mile to the Lower Falls picnic area, and then park for free. If there's too much snow on the road, you may have to park on the side of the road and snowshoe to the trailhead.

The trek's starting point is Lower Falls of the McCloud River, which is some 40 feet wide with a 15-foot vertical chute. It forms a foamy avalanche of white suds that pour into a 25-yard-long pool. Fishermen and picnickers recline along the granite slab field overlooking the tantalizing scene.

Follow the wide asphalt path that traces the river upstream. Your snowprints may be the first along this isolated journey in winter and early spring. Douglas fir, occasional incense cedar, and white fir offer unwelcome shade but admirable evergreen foliage. Manzanita and ceanothus shrubs highlight the sunnier sections. Capture frequent views along the swift and icy clear McCloud River.

Reach Fowlers Camp Campground at 0.2 mile, a place where Wintu Indians seasonally camped to hunt and fish. Black oak, dogwood, and hazelnut display their bare branches starting at 0.4 mile. Spot a snow-free, eroded steep cliff on the other side of the river at 0.8 mile, and look for the 20-foot-tall, rare Pacific yew conifer at trailside. It features a peeling, madronelike trunk with redwood-like needles. Shortly, you'll see, but not hear, a charging sheet of white just beyond a big rock so imposing that it forces the course of the river to veer.

Gouged in a precipitous and rocky canyon laced with large Douglas firs, rectangular Middle Falls of the McCloud River range some 30 yards wide with an awesome drop-off half that distance. When a north breeze stirs, the chilly mist is invigorating in your face.

The route snakes up and away, reaches a prime vista down on the falls, and culminates on a rocky rim interspersed with manzanita. There's a clear view of the falls from a nearby granite rock perch beneath some ponderosa pines. The views here of Mount Shasta and the Trinity Divide mountains will be more in your face on the return journey.

Longing looks way down into the charging river continue for another 0.25 mile or so. Reach a shady section at 1.4 miles featuring a staggeringly steep wall of lichen-coated gray rock on the left side of your route. The initial sighting of the Upper Falls of the McCloud River promptly ensues just past this 20-foot-high corridor.

Hemmed in on both sides by stark, granitic, sheer walls, these falls are an extremely forceful chute of pure white water. Looking down on the surging water, it's easy to envision a bursting dam. Wander over to the falls' lip, where you'll be mesmerized by the 100-yard-long, all-white cascade speeding to plunge over the edge.

--58--
Forks of the Sacramento River to Gumboot Lake

Total distance: 22 miles
Hiking time: 2 days
Difficulty: Moderate
Elevation gain: 3,200 feet
High point: 6,400 feet
Maps: USGS Seven Lakes, USGS Mumbo Basin
Information: Mount Shasta Ranger District, Shasta-Trinity National Forest

The South and Middle Forks of the Sacramento River are an angler's dream in fishing season and a snowshoer's paradise in winter. Most of this remote and isolated snowshoe route allows you to look down on this highest stretch of the icy clear Upper Sacramento River as it bounds over boulders and rinses

South Fork of the Sacramento River

rock slabs. You'll have so many close-up views of pristine pools, frothy rapids, charging cascades, and mini-falls that you might have to factor in more time for taking extra photos. The numerous views eastward of Mounts Shasta and Shastina will likely use up some film on partly cloudy or clear days.

This is a little-known course even to cross-country skiers, and chances are you'll have this winter wonderland to yourself, although rarely a snowmobiler may careen by, especially on weekends. Following the route is simple, since it's the snow-covered Forest Road 26, which is plowed by Siskiyou County to the

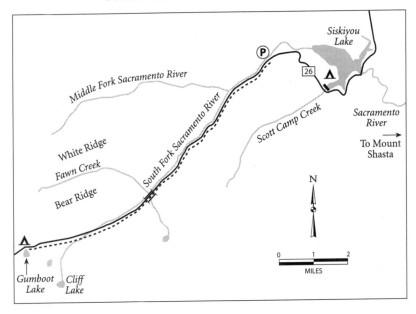

forest boundary. This allows ardent and prepared trekkers to proceed in a light snowstorm.

Most snowshoers just mosey up the trail a mile or two, gawk at the river a couple dozen times, and then head back, which is certainly a good option. Call ahead to determine if there's enough snow to deem this a snowshoe route. If not, consider Route 60 to Heart Lake.

Leave I-5 at the Central Mount Shasta exit and head west and south on South Old Stage Road and W.A. Barr Road. Cross the dam at Siskiyou Lake 2.6 miles from the freeway exit, then continue on the road (now called Forest Road 26) to about 2 miles west of Lake Siskiyou Camp Resort. Park for free along the road, but do not block traffic, because four-wheel-drive vehicles access this road, although rarely. There is limited room for cars to get turned around, so park carefully.

The trip starts out mostly level, with clusters of greenleaf manzanita and huckleberry oak shrubs in open areas and incense cedar, Douglas fir, bigleaf maples, and ponderosa pines in the surrounding forest. In a clearing at 0.5 mile, there's an ideal view north of Mount Eddy. For the next couple of miles, the river is wide and charging along the north side of the road, covered with boulders and laced with alder shrubs and a few juvenile Douglas firs in high and drier spots.

At 2.5 miles, the river suddenly narrows at the confluence of the Middle Fork. For the next few miles, you'll have red-tailed-hawk's-eye views down on the South Fork of the Sacramento River on your left. The boulders are now several times the size of the boulders seen near the start, as the climb switches from gentle to moderate. Be sure to look behind to catch your breath and admire Mounts Shasta and Shastina.

At 7.4 miles, cross the bridge over Fawn Creek, which is a good picnic spot and turnaround point for all-day trekkers. The course now departs the river, and lodgepole pines, occasional sugar pines, and white firs become more frequent, accompanying you the rest of the way. Near the top of a rise about 1 mile farther, Forest Road 39N057 goes left for 1.5 miles to scenic Cliff Lake, a good side trip. The lake is semi-hemmed by a steep granite wall on its south side. The gradient gets a bit steeper over the final 2 miles to Gumboot Lake near the top of the Trinity Divide. This shallow lake is crowded in the summer, but arguably looks its best when snow-coated.

--*59*--

Castle Lake

Total distance: Up to 2–3 miles
Hiking time: 2–3 hours
Difficulty: Easy to moderate
Elevation gain: 300 feet
High point: 5,500 feet
Map: USGS Seven Lakes
Information: Mount Shasta Ranger District, Shasta-Trinity National Forest

During the usually lengthy snow season at Castle Lake, activity is brisk and varied and the scenery is splendid. Besides the rugged and remote beauty of this 47-acre alpine lake, snowshoers are apt to see avid fishermen casting through holes in the ice.

Occasionally, waggy-tailed dogs sprint across the ice or cross-country skiers visit this 120-foot-deep jewel. Rarely, a snowmobiler sojourns at this easily accessible winter wonderland.

Leave I-5 at the Central Mount Shasta exit and head west and south on South Old Stage Road and W.A. Barr Road. Cross the dam at Lake Siskiyou 2.6 miles from the freeway exit, then turn left 0.2 mile farther onto paved Castle

Castle Lake

Lake Road. Park for free in the spacious lot at road's end 7 miles past Castle Lake Campground.

Though the snowshoe routes on and around Castle Lake are numerous, the suggested course is up and back along the west then south shores. You'll encounter fewer folks this way, and see more gorgeous scenery. The trip can be lengthened by wandering out onto the ice-coated lake whenever you fancy— just check carefully to ensure the ice and snow easily supports you. If ice skaters are zipping around the lake effortlessly, it's probably safe.

Be sure to read the useful signboards at the north end that discuss the fish, geology, and natural and human history of the lake. Then off you go, heading counterclockwise, crossing the outlet and traversing along the shapely shoreline and soon past the UC Davis research station. The deciduous twigs all around are western azaleas, which thrive beneath slender and upright red firs and lodgepole pines. In more open sections, note the profusion of greenleaf manzanita and bush chinquapin. As you approach the stark, granite cliffs on the south shore, there's a rocky perch—ideal for gazing toward the castlelike stone wall for seasonal waterfalls, which may resemble huge, frozen icicles.

As with all glacial cirques (semicircular lakes), Castle Lake is by far the deepest near its steep stone wall. The lake was formed more than 10,000 years ago when much of Northern California was covered in glaciers. The Shasta and Wintu Indians called it "Castle of the Devil." They believed that the evil spirit "Ku-Ku-Pa-Rick" dwelled deep in the lake and made eerie noises usually heard in the winter. This moaning (listen for it) is now thought to be movement of ice on the lake's surface.

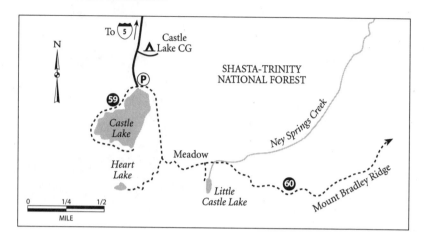

To gain improved views, simply scamper up the west or northern slope a bit, or take at least the strenuous start of Route 60 if time and energy permit.

--60--

Heart Lake and Mount Bradley Ridge

Total distance: 7 miles or longer; 1.8 miles for Heart Lake
Hiking time: 4 hours or 2 days
Difficulty: Moderate
Elevation gain: 1,300 feet
High point: 6,050 feet
Maps: USGS Dunsmuir, USGS Seven Lakes
Information: Mount Shasta Ranger District, Shasta-Trinity National Forest

Magical Mount Shasta is full of good vibes that beckon harmonic convergence. This ramble reveals several special views of the shiny, snow-coated mountain. It's a rare treat to gaze down on snow-covered Castle Lake, with snow-free Black Butte backed by snow-clad Mount Shasta. Another view bonus includes Lassen Peak beyond a bevy of jagged rock outcrops called Castle Crags. How about Lake Siskiyou and the Mount Shasta valley adorned with Mount Shasta?

Navigational and routefinding skills will surely come in handy for this journey, which can easily be abbreviated by exploring around Heart Lake, then coming back. In some situations (such as mid-spring), you may have to lug your snowshoes over random snowdrifts to get to deeper snowpack. Occasionally, after a heavy snow, you may have to park 0.5 mile or more below the trailhead. Call ahead to check on snow conditions.

Leave I-5 at the Central Mount Shasta exit and head west and south on South Old Stage Road and W.A. Barr Road. Cross the dam at Lake Siskiyou 2.6 miles from the freeway exit, then turn left 0.2 mile farther onto paved Castle Lake Road. Park for free in the spacious lot at road's end at 7 miles.

Arguably, the steepest and riskiest snowshoeing of the entire trip happens soon after crossing a small stream, when you pick and choose your way upslope and along the eastern banks of Castle Lake. Hopefully, someone who's been this route before has laid tracks. Ascend in an open forest, where snow weighs down evergreen huckleberry oak and deciduous western ninebark shrubs. Plan on stopping frequently at well-chosen vantage points to take a breather, cool down, and peer down upon Castle Lake.

Reach a rocky saddle 0.6 mile into the route, bear right (south), and head for the snow meadow. Nestled in a rocky basin just above, pristine and tiny

View of Black Butte from Heart Lake

Heart Lake awaits at 1 mile. Imagine what the boulder-laced shoreline and surrounding ground covers of mountain spiraea and red mountain heather would look like after the snow melts. Negotiate your way to a clear spot just above the lake from the south side, and snap some photos of the lake backed by majestic Mount Shasta. Add Black Butte and Castle Lake to this striking scene by ambling over to the lake's boulder-clogged outlet. Wander westward past a couple of makeshift campsites to the safe side of a sheer and dark cliff face gazing down on Castle Lake.

To access view-laden Mount Bradley Ridge, retrace your tracks, then continue east to the lowest part of the gap. Descend steeply past regal red firs to a meadow at 2.4 miles. Soon after, cross Ney Springs Creek and begin a pick-and-choose ascent southeast of Mount Bradley Ridge. At the top (3.1 miles), a snow-covered old forest road makes for easy snowshoeing eastward for up to several miles. By scrambling to the north, you'll gain staggering views of Mount Shasta, Lake Siskiyou, and Mount Eddy. Views straight ahead include forest-shrouded Girard Ridge in the forefront, with Lassen Peak, Crater Peak, Clover Mountain, and Snow Mountain stretching from south to north in the distance. Watch for Mount Bradley Lookout straight ahead along this mostly flat route. Find a vantage point past manzanita and bush chinquapin to the south for spying Castle Crags.

--61--

Cascade Gulch

Total distance: 5 miles
Hiking time: 5–7 hours
Difficulty: Moderate for the first 1.5 miles; strenuous the last mile
Elevation gain: 2,000 feet
High point: 6,800 feet
Map: USGS City of Mount Shasta
Information: Mount Shasta Ranger District, Shasta-Trinity National Forest

Think of Cascade Gulch as sort of an unofficial, backdoor entry to the flanks of Mount Shasta, an ideal access to isolated backcountry that few folks know. Ah, but herein lies the true beauty of this trip. Peaceful and remote, this mixed conifer forest trek is a superb alternative to other nearby Mount Shasta area routes in this book. In fact, a snowshoer could do the first half or so of this journey (easy to moderate), then add another route the same day higher up

Mount Shasta from Cascade Gulch

the mountain. Cross-country skiers sometimes get dropped off at Bunny Flat, then ski down to the bottom portion of Cascade Gulch, cutting over to its trailhead for pickup. Snowshoers can certainly opt for this 2.5-mile ramble as well.

Starting at 4,800 feet in elevation, this may be the only route available on the mountain during times of heavy snow when Everitt Memorial Highway remains to be plowed. Then again, it may be the only route closed later in spring after melt-off. You may see a few cross-country skiers along the way, perhaps a dog or two, and rarely a snowmobiler. For sure, you'll see unique views of Mount Shasta, Black Butte, and Mount Eddy, unless low clouds are about.

From I-5, take the Central Mount Shasta exit and follow the main street east toward Mount Shasta—it eventually becomes Everitt Memorial Highway as it bends north. From the first crossing of the railroad tracks downtown, it's a scenic and winding 5-mile drive to the junction of Forest Road 41N56 (your route), where you park for free on the right side of the highway. There's usually

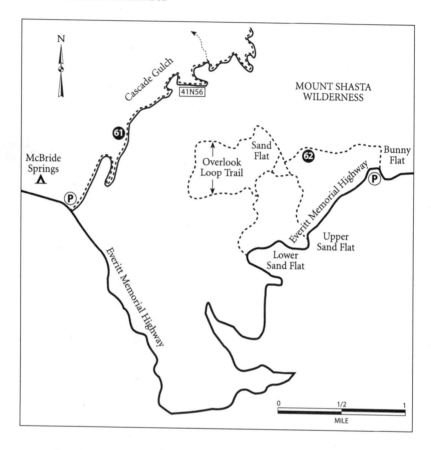

room for about six vehicles here. When you drive past McBride Springs Campground, it's another 0.25 mile to the trailhead.

The route begins totally flat for the first 0.5 mile or so, heading straight for Shastina Mountain. The view of this 12,330-foot sidekick of Mount Shasta takes center stage and deserves a few photos. A continuous grove of manzanita accompanies you at first, with white firs, ponderosa pines, and incense cedars poking through.

Chaparral declines rapidly as climbing resumes via a couple of switchbacks up Cascade Gulch. The next mile or so is spent ascending moderately in a tall, mixed forest. Occasional glimpses of Mount Shasta are detected through the conifer limbs. You'll notice the westward views of Black Butte and Mount Eddy through occasional clearings on the return route.

When you reach a junction at 1.7 miles, you can head back or forge forward by hanging a right and commencing an even steeper climb up Cascade Gulch.

--*62*--

Sand Flat and the Overlook Loop Trail

Total distance: 4.5 miles
Hiking time: 3–5 hours
Difficulty: Moderate
Elevation gain: 700 feet
High point: 6,900 feet
Map: USGS McCloud
Information: Mount Shasta Ranger District, Shasta-Trinity National Forest

Find out firsthand how a pair of neighboring dry meadows features substantially differing but amazing views with this unique route amid Shasta red firs. The views at first from Bunny Flat are north, straight up the imposing flanks of 14,162-foot-tall Mount Shasta. At the trek's destination, the westernmost section of the Overlook Loop Trail, the scenes switch to the west, where several vantage points afford souls with far-reaching views, including Mount Eddy and Black Butte. In between, there's Sand Flat, with alternative views all over, depending on which corner of the meadow you've snowshoed to.

Of course, you could park at Upper or Lower Sand Flat parking areas and skip the wide open views of Mount Shasta and Shastina from Bunny Flat, but that would be like listening to only part of a favorite song. The price of this route is that you get stuck with the bulk of the climbing at the finale, but it's well worth it. Probably by the time you reunite with Bunny Flat at journey's end, the crazy clouds that tend to convene around Mount Shasta will look strikingly different than at the start.

This is a trip filled with solitude, for once you leave families, snowman builders, and snowboarders behind at Bunny Flat, you're likely to encounter only an occasional cross-country skier or snowshoer.

From I-5, take the Central Mount Shasta exit and follow the main street east toward Mount Shasta—it eventually becomes Everitt Memorial Highway as it bends north. From the first crossing of the railroad tracks downtown, it's a scenic and winding 12.5-mile drive to the large and paved lot at Bunny Flat, where you park for free.

Head north from the west side of Bunny Flat, following the same tracks as those heading for Helen Lake. After 0.2 mile, look for the blue diamonds on the Shasta red firs that mark the way down to Sand Flat. Blue diamonds will help you stay on course the entire way if there are no previously laid tracks. At

1 mile, bear right at a junction from the east end of Sand Flat. Follow the tracks/blue diamonds north by northwest, keeping just to the right of a small, forested knob. The route bends westward at 1.3 miles, showing off densely forested Cascade Gulch nearby to the northwest below.

The level section of this route begins showing better views of Mount Shasta behind you as you reach the west end of Sand Flat at 1.8 miles. The following 0.5 mile on the Overlook Loop Trail heads south along the west corner of the flat, displaying numerous views of the Shasta Valley below to the west. Spot scenic Lake Siskiyou and a series of stark granite spires called Castle Crags. From out of nowhere, these minidomes and minarets rise abruptly from a peaceful forest, looking wonderfully out of place.

Straight ahead to the west stands smooth and snowy Mount Eddy, easily the second-tallest mountain in the area at 9,025 feet. Dark gray and usually snowless, Black Butte caps the Shasta Valley. This young plug-dome volcano formed just less than 10,000 years ago when four separate eruptions squeezed thick, viscous lava 2,300 feet above the surrounding plain. For photos, show

Fog surrounds Black Butte, seen from Sand Flat

up in midmorning when sunlight strikes these two mountains brightly and dramatic shadows are still cast across the forest and valley.

The Overlook Loop Trail now swings east for 0.5 mile, connecting with Lower Sand Flat Road, where you veer left, followed by another left 0.2 mile farther. Hang a right 200 yards farther at 3.7 miles as you now retrace your footprints, only steadily uphill to Bunny Flat.

--*63*--
Helen Lake and Mount Shasta

Total distance: 7 miles to Helen Lake; 12 miles to Mount Shasta summit
Hiking time: 7 hours for Helen Lake; 2 days for Mount Shasta summit
Difficulty: Strenuous
Elevation gain: 3,300 feet for Helen Lake; 7,300 feet for Mount
    Shasta summit
High point: 14,162 feet
Maps: USGS Mount Shasta, USGS McCloud
Information: Mount Shasta Ranger District, Shasta-Trinity National Forest

Laden with so much snow, Mount Shasta by late winter looks as though it's eternally clothed in white. The massive mountain seems to possess magic, gleaming invitingly on sunny days and looming ominously when clouds try to get in the way. Towering 10,000 feet above surrounding terrain to dominate Northern California, this crowning rampart of the Cascade Range draws folks from around the world. Native American Indians have long believed that Mount Shasta envelops special spiritual powers, and they felt its healing power through song, dance, and prayer.

This classic and least difficult of all routes up the mountain offers two goals. If you're fit, patient, and committed, claim the summit and boost your self-esteem forever. If you're inspired to savor some harmonic convergence simply by trekking partway up these dramatic slopes, you can always say with a satisfied smile, "I once went climbing on Mount Shasta."

The higher you climb, the more you'll need careful planning, proper equipment, and supplies. You'll also need to fill out a free wilderness permit at Bunny Flat trailhead if you're going beyond Horse Camp. Snowshoers spending the night at Helen Lake must purchase a summit pass (good above 10,000 feet in elevation) by using the self-issue fee envelope at Bunny Flat. Be ready for extreme weather conditions and/or rapidly changing weather. Always check

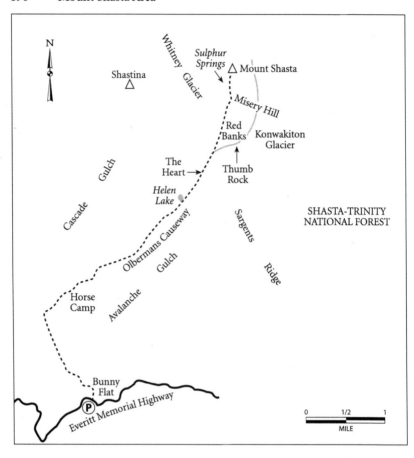

the Forest Service avalanche advisory and the latest forecast ahead of time. If you're proceeding up Avalanche Gulch and beyond, consider saving this snowshoe trip for late spring or early summer, when it's much safer.

From I-5, take the Central Mount Shasta exit and follow the main street east toward Mount Shasta—it eventually becomes Everitt Memorial Highway as it bends north. From the first crossing of the railroad tracks downtown, it's a scenic and winding 12.5-mile drive to the large and paved lot at Bunny Flat, where you park for free.

To start, traipse slowly across Bunny Flat, partly to warm up and partly to fully gather the photogenic south-facing views of the mountain. Mount Shasta is a stratovolcano that has erupted four times over the last 250,000 years. The last eruption was 200 years ago. Five prominent glaciers ring the mountain,

Red fir and Mount Shasta

with part of Whitney Glacier viewable from Bunny Flat just west of the summit and most of Wintun Glacier seen to the east of the top. Bunny Flat is the best spot on the route to capture the south face of Shastina Mountain to the west of Mount Shasta, and the artistic form of Avalanche Gulch and the pointed expanses of Sargents Ridge along the south flank of Mount Shasta.

Start climbing from the west end of Bunny Flat (a dry meadow in summer) in a Shasta red fir forest. The Sierra Club cabin (historic stone cabin that is off-limits for overnighters except for an emergency) and meadow of Horse Camp is reached at 1.8 miles. This scenic area makes for an ideal camping spot or a turnaround destination for snowshoers short on time and/or energy.

The climb resumes up Olbermans Causeway, which ends near tree line. Utilize routefinding skills to access the west side of Avalanche Gulch and soon climb to Helen Lake at 3.5 miles. A flat snowfield situated at 10,443 feet elevation, Helen Lake shows off imposing Thumb Rock above to the north and jagged Sargents Ridge to the east. This is another superb camping area or turnaround point.

Heavy-duty climbing ensues as you sweat and swear your way up Avalanche Gulch. At this high of altitude, now is the time to plod along slowly the rest of the way to reduce the effects of altitude sickness, which you might experience. The route gets even steeper as you approach The Heart at 12,000 feet elevation. Head right and go for the gap between Thumb Rock and the Red Banks. Climb steadily past Konwakiton Glacier to the right and the Red Banks on your left. If the snow is packed, it's probably best to switch to crampons and ice ax.

If you made it past the Red Banks, the next challenge is Misery Hill, which starts at 13,000 feet elevation and rises to 13,800 feet to a flat area for a chance to breathe the thin air deeply. With the hard part behind, continue north and pass just east of Sulphur Springs, which helped keep John Muir from freezing to death. Save the worshipping until you've mounted the summit by heading briefly east, then scramble madly to the top.

Guess what? The views are inexplicable, except to say they're amazing. Lassen Peak is backed by the Sierra Nevada way off in the southern distance. Heading clockwise, the Sacramento Valley and Coast Range seem to march forever, and the rocky spires of the Klamath Mountains dazzle to the west. More Cascade Mountains impress to the north.

--*64*--
Panther Meadows and Old Ski Bowl

Total distance: 4.6 miles
Hiking time: 4–6 hours
Difficulty: Moderate
Elevation gain: 1,100 feet
High point: 7,800 feet
Map: USGS McCloud
Information: Mount Shasta Ranger District, Shasta-Trinity National Forest

Snow-covered meadows invite a peaceful, spiritual feeling, especially at a place full of views called Panther Meadows. Sacred to many Native Americans, a subalpine meadow such as this is rare on Mount Shasta because the porous volcanic soil doesn't retain water near the surface. However, springs such as Panther Springs feed Panther Meadows, allowing native grasses and wildflowers to flourish amidst the stones beneath the winter and spring snow coat.

Crammed with incredible views the whole way, this route follows snow-covered Everitt Memorial Highway to its terminus at the Old Ski Bowl, which was slammed by a tremendous avalanche in 1995 that swept down thousands

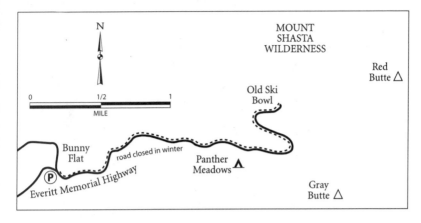

of feet to near Panther Meadows. Call ahead for the latest report on avalanche conditions. The course passes through an open Shasta red fir forest featuring firs of all sizes and shapes, then becomes virtually treeless beyond Panther Meadows.

On brisk and sunny weekends, you may greet a few cross-country skiers and perhaps a dog or snowmobiler. As soon as you round the first bend climbing away mildly from Bunny Flat, utter seclusion and tranquility awaits.

From I-5, take the Central Mount Shasta exit and follow the main street east toward Mount Shasta—it eventually becomes Everitt Memorial Highway as it bends north. From the first crossing of the railroad tracks downtown, it's a scenic and winding 12.5-mile drive to the large and paved lot at Bunny Flat, where you park for free.

Gaze beyond Bunny Flat and capture the south face of Shastina Mountain to the west of Mount Shasta. Observe the artistic form of Avalanche Gulch and the pointed expanses of Sargents Ridge along the south flank of Mount Shasta. As you stride along your route eastward, Lassen Peak to the south appears frequently through clearings in the firs. Pause often to gather your breath and stare behind you to the west for awesome views of the snowy Trinity Divide range, backed by the Trinity Alps, whose caps are part snow and part granitic spires. The best photos to the west are taken on sunny mornings.

The route twists steadily upward, past erratic, large boulders encased in the upward slope, especially over the first mile. At 1.3 miles, the first unimpeded views of tree-clad Red Butte and Gray Butte to the east appear. Pass a campground on the right, then enter Panther Meadows at 1.6 miles. After some quality hang time here, continue on the snowy road east for 0.3 mile past mountain hemlocks and red firs, then note that the climb intensifies as you swing

Mount Shasta from near Panther Meadow

north toward Mount Shasta. By now the landscape is virtually treeless and views of Sargents Ridge and the east flank of Mount Shasta take center stage.

Reach the Old Ski Bowl at 2.3 miles and get set to take photos of the mountain and do some picnicking. Note that the journey can easily be increased by heading upslope.

--*65*--

Parks Creek Pass

Total distance: Up to 20 miles
Hiking time: 5 hours–2 days
Difficulty: Moderate
Elevation gain: 3,100 feet
High point: 6,800 feet
Maps: USGS South China Mountain, USGS Mount Eddy
Information: Mount Shasta Ranger District, Shasta-Trinity National Forest

Get numerous, uninterrupted views of volcanic domes adorning the Mount Shasta Valley, which contrasts superbly with the countless views of metamorphic mountains, such as Mount Eddy, on this isolated, little-known snowshoe route

200

northwest of Mount Shasta. Add the sightings of largely granitic Trinity Alps spires and this makes for a wondrous and varied geological excursion.

Because you'll climb incessantly but moderately through forests and chaparral, past flats and clearings, and over slopes and canyons, you're bound to get in tune with wildlife along narrow and twisting, snow-covered Parks Creek Road. Great horned owls may be watching you with their catlike eyes while hidden in the firs. While taking one of your many breathers, watch for a warbler darting amidst the lower branches of Douglas firs and ponderosa pines. Listen for the ceaseless knocking of the woodpecker drilling into a white fir trunk, and watch for the conspicuous mountain chickadee, sometimes acrobatically hanging upside down, boldly and actively foraging in front of you. Peer down the canyons for a chance sighting of a wily coyote trotting in a clearing.

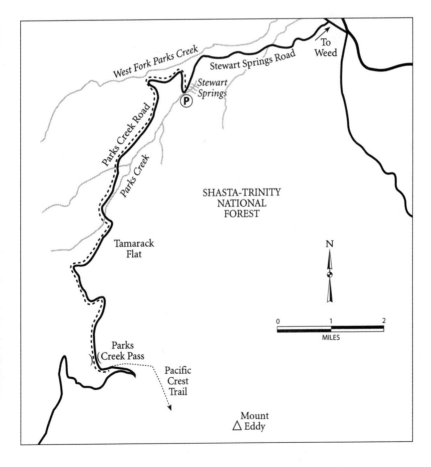

If abbreviated, this can be an easy trek for novice snowshoers who ascend the easy-to-follow road along the west side of Parks Creek Canyon until time and/or energy compels a turnaround. If climbed all or most of the way, the return route becomes an awesome thrill ride for cross-country skiers or crazed souls willing to lug snowboards.

If the snow line is a bit higher than the starting point, consider carrying your snowshoes to a point with enough snow, or opt for Routes 59 or 60 to Castle and Heart Lakes. Call ahead for snow conditions. Because the varying views are frequent and inspirational, do this trip on a clear or partly cloudy day. The ultimate journey would be a clear day after a light snow, when the conifer boughs are slightly bent with powder. Rarely do snowmobilers use this route.

To get there, take I-5's Edgewood/Gazelle exit just north of Weed. Drive under the freeway, turn right at the stop sign, and then travel 0.3 mile farther and turn left onto signed Stewart Springs Road. Drive about 3 miles to the junction of Stewart Springs Road and Parks Creek Road (Forest Road 17) and park for free on the side of the plowed road. If Parks Creek Road is snow-free, you can drive on to the snow line, thus shortening your hike.

The trip begins minus the anticipated views in an open forest of oaks and ponderosa pines. But at 1.2 miles from the Stewarts Spring Road and Parks Creek Road junction, the snow-covered road veers south, allowing for views several miles to the east of grayish brown volcanic domes dotting the Mount Shasta Valley to the north of out-of-view Mount Shasta.

Vistas continue through clearings of Douglas firs and incense cedars as you reach Tamarack Flat 4 miles farther. By now, glimpses of the shoulder of metamorphic Mount Eddy to the southeast appear sporadically, and soon there are occasional close-up views to the west of unnamed metamorphic peaks and slopes featuring profuse segments of sometimes snow-free loose talus.

If timed right, the relentless climb can be frequently rewarded with pause-and-refresh views to the east or west, past scattered clusters of manzanita, chinquapin, and huckleberry oak shrubs in an open forest where white firs enter the scene.

At 4.8 miles past Tamarack Flat, reach view-laden Parks Creek Pass. The best photos are to the southwest of the jagged, snow-clad Trinity Alps. The pass doubles as the trailhead for Deadfall Lakes, a mere 2.5 miles of gentle climbing to the southeast via the Pacific Crest Trail. Those with advanced navigational and mountaineering skills can venture further to this trio of snowbound lakes.

Red firs frame the moon

--66--

Callahan Lava Flow and Whitney Butte

Total distance: 7.2 miles
Hiking time: 4–5 hours
Difficulty: Moderate
Elevation gain: 600 feet
High point: 5,000 feet
Maps: USGS Lava Beds National Monument or free park map at visitor center
Information: Lava Beds National Monument

Snowshoe peacefully in a sacred land that at least metaphysically still belongs to the Modoc Indians. They were massacred here in a terrible war in 1872, but their memories and spirits seem to linger over Lava Beds National Monument. You're invited to reflect on this while snowshoeing the same territory the Modoc Indians roamed, which is just a few lava stone's throws away from an actual battle site.

Your route has a miles-from-nowhere feel, starting at Merrill Ice Cave, one of several you can easily explore while at Lava Beds National Monument. Early winter's an ideal time to look for large mule deer near the trail. When there's snow here, it can sometimes look like a cross between a sci-fi movie and a photo negative. Bring a camera to capture this mostly flat but bumpy land in front of Mount Shasta from a rare vantage point from the east. Red-tailed hawks sometimes soar above the many piles of bumpy rocks, which resemble snow pillows after a good snowstorm. This is a land where the eerie echoes of howling coyotes still occur after dark.

Expect to see few folks in the winter, but you may encounter a cross-country skier or two along the way. The easy-to-follow route isn't always snow-covered in winter, so call ahead to determine if there is enough.

Drive Highway 299 East to Canby (133 miles from Redding). Turn north on Highway 139, drive 20 miles, and then turn west on paved Lava Beds National Monument Road. Reach the Visitor Center after a few miles, continue 2.1 miles, turn west at the sign for Merrill Ice Cave, and then park in the lot when this paved road dead ends 0.9 mile farther.

The wide open route first heads mostly north through a flat and grayish desert motif of low-growing shrubs. California sage dominates, but there's also bitterbrush, rabbit brush, and occasional mountain mahogany. Western junipers come in all sizes here, from waist high to 10-yard-tall stand-alone specimens.

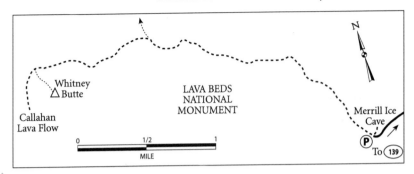

An array of odd-shaped and geologically intriguing cinder cones, buttes, and domed peaks accentuate the snowy countryside in all directions. With this mix of low shrubs and lava rock clusters, one moment you can feel like you're hauntingly in the middle of the Nevada desert, the next moment is like moon exploration.

Several room-sized lava rock boulders coated with crustose lichens appear closely on the right at 1.7 miles. Choose one to scramble up and acquire a spectacular panorama. Note the striking contrast of two angular mountains—Shasta (west) and McLoughlin (north)—with the area's scattered domes, cones, and buttes.

Elongated, dome-shaped Whitney Butte is enticingly close here, beckoning to be conquered. A westward view of Mount Shasta is precious and unique, accentuated here with the linear rim stretching below Whitney Butte's southern flank. Checking out this scene at sunset is pure heaven.

Continue snowshoeing and pause to marvel at an 18-foot-tall juniper with 4 feet of its bottom-most trunk completely encased in large lava rocks. Go left at a trail fork at 2.2 miles and then round Whitney Butte 1 mile farther. The trail soon ends at Lava Beds National Monument's largest and most impressive sheet of basalt—Callahan Lava Flow. Covering many square miles, this bumpy field of dark gray boulders was extruded from Cinder Butte to the south more than 1000 years ago. The snow lingers on these rocks a very short time.

To climb Whitney Butte (a cinder cone), double-back 100 yards or so, then pick and choose your way a couple hundred feet to the summit, scattered with conifers and superb views in all directions. Look east and north and admire Gillem Bluff and Schonchin Butte. They both can be easily reached after short hikes—about 1 mile. Obtain a free map from the visitor center.

Back at your car, grab a flashlight and follow the numerous steps down into Merrill Ice Cave to eventually reach an ice lake. Frozen year-round, cold air sinks into the cave in winter and freezes the water. There's a labyrinth of caves at the visitor center and several others on the map of this park.

West Prospect Peak along Baker Lake route

Information

Amador Ranger District, Eldorado National Forest
26820 Silver Drive
Pioneer, CA 95666
(209) 295-4251

Eldorado National Forest
3070 Camino Heights Drive
Camino, CA 95709
(530) 644-6048

Emerald Bay State Park
P.O. Box 266
Tahoma, CA 96142
(530) 525-7277
www.agency.resources.ca.gov/parks/dpr.html

Hat Creek Ranger District
Lassen National Forest
P.O. Box 220
Fall River Mills, CA 96028
(530) 336-5521

Inyo National Forest
Mono Lake Ranger District
P.O. Box 429
Lee Vining, CA 93541
(760) 647-3000

Lake Tahoe Basin Management Unit
870 Emerald Bay Road, Suite 1
South Lake Tahoe, CA 96150
(530) 573-2674

Lassen Volcanic National Park
P.O. Box 100
Mineral, CA 96063-0100
(530) 595-4444
www.nps.gov/lavol

McCloud Ranger District
Shasta-Trinity National Forest
P.O. Box 1620
McCloud, CA 96057
(530) 964-2184

Mount Shasta Ranger District
Shasta-Trinity National Forest
204 West Alma
Mount Shasta, CA 96067
(530) 926-4511
www.r5.fs.fed.us/shasta trinity/mt.shasta/

Tahoe National Forest
631 Coyote Street
Nevada City, CA 95959-6003
(530) 265-4531 or (530) 587-3558
www.r5.fs.fed.us/tahoe/

Toiyabe National Forest, Bridgeport Ranger District
P.O. Box 595
Bridgeport, CA 93517
(760) 932-7070

Yosemite National Park
CA 95389-0577
1-800-208-2434, (209) 372-0200
www.nps.gov/yose/

Quick Trail Reference

Kings Creek and Lassen Peak

EASTERN SIERRA NEVADA
Highway 395 from Tioga Pass Area to Sonora Pass

	WATER AND ICE FEATURES	MAGICAL MEADOW	INTERESTING ROCK FORMATIONS	INTERESTING TREE SPECIMENS	AWESOME VIEWS	CROSS-COUNTRY SKI OPTION	FAMILY OUTING	BIRDWATCHING	PAY SITE
1. Minaret Vista and San Joaquin Ridge					•	•	•		
2. Burgers Animal Sanctuary		•	•	•	•	•			
3. Lundy Lake to Oneida Lake	•				•				
4. Lundy Canyon	•		•						
5. Virginia Lakes	•			•		•	•		
6. Robinson Creek to Barney Lake	•								
7. Twin Lakes	•				•	•	•	•	
8. Pickel Meadow	•	•			•	•	•		
9. Leavitt Meadow: Poore Lake and Secret Lake	•	•			•	•	•	•	

WESTERN SIERRA NEVADA   *Yosemite Valley Area from Highway 41 to Highway 120*

	WATER AND ICE FEATURES	MAGICAL MEADOW	INTERESTING ROCK FORMATIONS	INTERESTING TREE SPECIMENS	AWESOME VIEWS	CROSS-COUNTRY SKI OPTION	FAMILY OUTING	BIRDWATCHING	PAY SITE
10. Badger Pass to Glacier Point		•			•	•			•
11. Ostrander Lake			•			•			•

WESTERN SIERRA NEVADA *Continued*
Yosemite Valley Area from Highway 41 to Highway 120

	WATER AND ICE FEATURES	MAGICAL MEADOW	INTERESTING ROCK FORMATIONS	INTERESTING TREE SPECIMENS	AWESOME VIEWS	CROSS-COUNTRY SKI OPTION	FAMILY OUTING	BIRDWATCHING	PAY SITE
12. Tempo Dome and Westfall Meadows		•		•					•
13. Mirror Lake and Tenaya Creek		•	•						•
14. Yosemite Valley: Yosemite Falls and Royal Arches		•	•		•	•	•		•
15. Yosemite Valley: El Capitan and Bridalveil Falls		•	•		•	•	•		•
16. Inspiration Point and Stanford Point					•				•
17. Tuolumne Grove and Hodgdon Meadow		•		•	•				•
18. Crane Flat Lookout						•			•
19. Merced Grove				•		•			•

NORTHERN SIERRA NEVADA *Carson Pass Area near Highway 88*

	WATER AND ICE FEATURES	MAGICAL MEADOW	INTERESTING ROCK FORMATIONS	INTERESTING TREE SPECIMENS	AWESOME VIEWS	CROSS-COUNTRY SKI OPTION	FAMILY OUTING	BIRDWATCHING	PAY SITE
20. Silver Lake	•		•	•		•		•	
21. Caples Lake and Emigrant Lake	•							•	
22. Little Round Top				•	•				•

NORTHERN SIERRA NEVADA *Continued*
Carson Pass Area near Highway 88

Trail	Water and Ice Features	Magical Meadow	Interesting Rock Formations	Interesting Tree Specimens	Awesome Views	Cross-Country Ski Option	Family Outing	Birdwatching	Pay Site
23. Upper Truckee River and Meiss Lake	•	•		•					•
24. Red Lake Peak					•				•
25. Crater Lake	•			•					
26. Scotts Lake and Waterhouse Peak		•	•		•				
27. Big Meadow and Round Lake	•	•						•	

LAKE TAHOE AREA *From Highway 50 to Highway 80*

Trail	Water and Ice Features	Magical Meadow	Interesting Rock Formations	Interesting Tree Specimens	Awesome Views	Cross-Country Ski Option	Family Outing	Birdwatching	Pay Site
28. Echo Lakes	•								
29. Becker Peak					•				
30. Angora Lookout and Angora Lakes	•			•	•				
31. Fallen Leaf Lake	•	•	•		•	•	•	•	
32. Mount Tallac			•		•				
33. Eagle Point and Emerald Bay	•				•	•	•	•	

LAKE TAHOE AREA *Continued*
From Highway 50 to Highway 80

	PAY SITE	BIRDWATCHING	FAMILY OUTING	CROSS-COUNTRY SKI OPTION	AWESOME VIEWS	INTERESTING TREE SPECIMENS	INTERESTING ROCK FORMATIONS	MAGICAL MEADOW	WATER AND ICE FEATURES
34. Meeks Creek			•	•				•	•
35. Blackwood Canyon to Barker Pass	•			•		•			
36. Loch Leven Lakes									
37. Donner Pass to Mount Judah					•		•		
38. Andesite Peak					•		•		
39. Castle Valley to Round Valley				•				•	
40. Castle Peak					•		•		

LASSEN VOLCANIC NATIONAL PARK AREA *Highway 36 to Highway 44*

	PAY SITE	BIRDWATCHING	FAMILY OUTING	CROSS-COUNTRY SKI OPTION	AWESOME VIEWS	INTERESTING TREE SPECIMENS	INTERESTING ROCK FORMATIONS	MAGICAL MEADOW	WATER AND ICE FEATURES
41. Susan River		•	•	•			•		•
42. Lake Almanor Recreation Trail		•	•	•					•
43. Nanny Creek						•	•		•
44. Ridge Lakes and Sulphur Works	•								•

LASSEN VOLCANIC NATIONAL PARK AREA
Highway 36 to Highway 44 *Continued*

	WATER AND ICE FEATURES	MAGICAL MEADOW	INTERESTING ROCK FORMATIONS	INTERESTING TREE SPECIMENS	AWESOME VIEWS	CROSS-COUNTRY SKI OPTION	FAMILY OUTING	BIRDWATCHING	PAY SITE
45. Lake Helen and Kings Creek Meadow	•	•			•	•		•	•
46. Cinder Cone and Fantastic Lava Beds			•		•				
47. Baker Lake and Hat Creek Rim			•	•		•			
48. Hat Creek Rim and Pacific Crest Trail			•		•				
49. Plum Valley			•	•		•			
50. Hat Creek	•			•					
51. West Prospect Peak					•	•			
52. Reflection Lake and Manzanita Lake	•					•	•	•	•
53. Manzanita Creek	•					•			•
54. Paradise Meadow	•	•							•
55. Crystal and Baum Lakes	•					•	•	•	

MOUNT SHASTA AREA
Around Interstate 5

	WATER AND ICE FEATURES	MAGICAL MEADOW	INTERESTING ROCK FORMATIONS	INTERESTING TREE SPECIMENS	AWESOME VIEWS	CROSS-COUNTRY SKI OPTION	FAMILY OUTING	BIRDWATCHING	PAY SITE
56. Castle Creek and Horse Heaven Meadow	•	•	•			•		•	
57. McCloud River Waterfalls	•						•		
58. Forks of the Sacramento River to Gumboot Lake	•		•			•			
59. Castle Lake	•					•	•		
60. Heart Lake and Mount Bradley Ridge	•			•	•				
61. Cascade Gulch				•					
62. Sand Flat and the Overlook Loop Trail		•			•				
63. Helen Lake and Mount Shasta					•				
64. Panther Meadows and Old Ski Bowl					•				
65. Parks Creek Pass	•				•	•			
66. Callahan Lava Flow and Whitney Butte			•	•	•	•			•

Lundy Lake and Lundy Creek Canyon

Index

About the Author

MARC J. SOARES is a landscape consultant and professional outdoor photographer and naturalist. He teaches plant and yoga classes for Shasta College Community Education and coaches the West Valley High School swim team. He also plays guitar and sings in a local classic rock band, and writes columns for the *Redding Record Searchlight* newspaper.

Marc has written four other hiking guidebooks: *100 Hikes in the San Francisco Bay Area* (The Mountaineers Books, 2001), *100 Classic Hikes in Northern California* (The Mountaineers Books, 2000; co-written with John R. Soares), *75 Year-Round Hikes in Northern California: The Ultimate Guide for Fall, Winter, and Spring Hikes* (The Mountaineers Books, 2000), and *Best Coast Hikes of Northern California: A Guide to the Top Trails from Big Sur to the Oregon Border* (Sierra Club, 1998).

THE MOUNTAINEERS, founded in 1906, is a nonprofit outdoor activity and conservation club, whose mission is "to explore, study, preserve, and enjoy the natural beauty of the outdoors. . . ." Based in Seattle, Washington, the club is now the third-largest such organization in the United States, with 15,000 members and five branches throughout Washington State.

The Mountaineers sponsors both classes and year-round outdoor activities in the Pacific Northwest, which include hiking, mountain climbing, ski-touring, snowshoeing, bicycling, camping, kayaking and canoeing, nature study, sailing, and adventure travel. The club's conservation division supports environmental causes through educational activities, sponsoring legislation, and presenting informational programs. All club activities are led by skilled, experienced volunteers, who are dedicated to promoting safe and responsible enjoyment and preservation of the outdoors.

If you would like to participate in these organized outdoor activities or the club's programs, consider a membership in The Mountaineers. For information and an application, write or call The Mountaineers, Club Headquarters, 300 Third Avenue West, Seattle, WA 98119; 206-284-6310.

The Mountaineers Books, an active, nonprofit publishing program of the club, produces guidebooks, instructional texts, historical works, natural history guides, and works on environmental conservation. All books produced by The Mountaineers Books fulfill the club's mission.

Send or call for our catalog of more than 500 outdoor titles:

The Mountaineers Books
1001 SW Klickitat Way, Suite 201
Seattle, WA 98134
800-553-4453
mbooks@mountaineersbooks.org
www.mountaineersbooks.org

The Mountaineers Books is proud to be a corporate sponsor of Leave No Trace, whose mission is to promote and inspire responsible outdoor recreation through education, research, and partnerships. The Leave No Trace program is focused specifically on human-powered (nonmotorized) recreation.

Leave No Trace strives to educate visitors about the nature of their recreational impacts, as well as offer techniques to prevent and minimize such impacts. Leave No Trace is best understood as an educational and ethical program, not as a set of rules and regulations.

For more information, visit *www.LNT.org*, or call 800-332-4100.

Other titles you might enjoy from The Mountaineers Books

Available at fine bookstores and outdoor stores, by phone at (800) 553-4453, or on the Web at www.mountaineersbooks.org

Snowshoeing: From Novice to Master, 5th Edition by Gene Prater and Dave Felkley. $16.95 paperbound. 0-89886-891-2.

Staying Alive in Avalanche Terrain by Bruce Tremper. $17.95 paperbound. 0-89886-834-3.

Glacier Travel & Crevasse Rescue, 2nd Edition by Andy Selters. $18.95 paperbound. 0-89886-658-8.

Wilderness Navigation: Finding Your Way Using Map, Compass, Altimeter, & GPS by Bob Burns and Mike Burns. $9.95 paperbound. 0-89886-629-4.

50 Classic Backcountry Ski & Snowboard Summits in California: Mount Shasta to Mount Whitney by Paul Richins Jr. $17.95 paperbound. 0-89886-656-1.

Free-Heel Skiing: Telemark and Parallel Techniques for All Conditions, 3rd Edition by Paul Parker. $19.95 paperbound. 0-89886-775-4.

100 Classic Hikes™ in Northern California, 2nd Edition by John R. Soares and Marc J. Soares. $19.95 paperbound. 0-89886-702-9.

Mountaineering: The Freedom of the Hills, 6th Edition by The Mountaineers, edited by Graydon and Hanson. $35.00 hardbound, 0-89886-426-7. $24.95 paperbound, 0-89886-427-5.

Conditioning for Outdoor Fitness: A Comprehensive Training Guide by David Musnick, M.D. and Mark Pierce, A.T.C. $21.95 paperbound. 0-89886-450-X.

Best Hikes with Children® in the San Francisco Bay Area, 2nd Edition by Bill and Kevin McMillon. $14.95 paperbound. 0-89886-786-X.

Best Hikes with Children® Around Sacramento by Bill McMillon. $12.95 paperbound. 0-89886-278-7.